MW00511424

"...we think that any reader who is ir sonal demons—or who wishes to he., invaluable." (Excerpt from Foreword)

Brad and Sherry Steiger
Authors, *Real Miracles, Divine Intervention,* and *Feats of Incredible Survival*

"It's refreshing to have an author acknowledge the need for 'proper spiritual training' for warriors entering into battle. Battles with demons: not only in the physical but on the spiritual planes as well. We must learn to use those weapons of 'energy, compassion, telepathy, and presence' as well as the physical tools at our disposal."

Officer Eric Saavedra, WPD
Crisis Intervention Specialist

"Tracee Dunblazier explains clearly how to not just avoid the frustrating, maddening, demoralizing demons that confront us in our lives but how to face them head-on, if and when we're ready, in no nonsense, self-supporting ways. Where these demons come from, what they want, and how to send them on their way are but the few things you'll discover in this fascinating read. The personal stories that represent Ms. Dunblazier's trials by fire from her own journey serve as valuable and moving lessons-learned for us all, presented with a clear-sighted, non-sentimental (yet profoundly touching) voice. Her emphasis on forgiveness and love is powerful, important, and belies a wisdom accrued from all the warriors captivatingly described within. A definite must-read!"

Stephen J. Miller
Author, *Keeper's of Mana'an*

"I LOVE this book! I thought it might be a little 'out there' even for me, but it's so practical and gives great realistic steps to battle negative energy. One week after trying Tracee's tips on humor, I'm feeling much more grounded at work. I can't wait to implement some of her other practical tips. I will be reading this book—and sections of this book—many times. It is profound!"

Sharon Kay King
Lifestyle blogger, Midlifemoments.me

"No matter where you start or what you bring, this book is enlightening, touching and empowering!! I love Tracee's open, non-judgmental and inclusive style that embraces the reader to pursue his / her own personal journey, while sharing in hers. Tracee's courage to share draws the reader in, and in turn, provides a sense of normalcy and strength to carry on, no matter the demons the reader may face. I love this book, and was sad when I finished it; can't wait to read volume II. Highly recommended!!"

Cristina Barbosa
Vancouver, Canada

Master Your Inner World

Embrace Your Power with Joy

*To Maron —
One of my favorite Demon Slayers on Earth*

Tracee Dunblazier

*Love Kate
2017*

GoTracee Publishing LLC

Baton Rouge, Louisiana Los Angeles, California

Copyright © 2016 Tracee Dunblazier

All rights reserved. No part of this book may be used or reproduced in any manner without the written permission of the publisher.

GoTracee Publishing LLC
240 Laurel Street, Suite 101
Baton Rouge, Louisiana, 70801
www.BeASlayer.com

ISBN: 978-0-9963907-4-3 print book
ISBN: 978-0-9963907-5-0 ebook

Illustrations: Michael J Penn www.michaeljpenn.com
Chakra Illustration Graphics: Tita Peterson
Cover & interior Design: Nelly Murariu www.PixBeeDesign.com
Editing: Eric Lyons Thomas, Kathleen Tracy

Disclaimer: Tracee Dunblazier is neither a medical doctor nor a mental health specialist, and does not offer medical diagnosis or therapy. No information and opinions offered through this title, through GoTracee Publishing LLC, or through any other venue representing Tracee Dunblazier are to be substituted for appropriate mental health or medical help. In no event are Tracee Dunblazier, her agents and/or representatives liable for any damages whatsoever arising out of or in any way connected with any individual's interpretation or use of information contained in this title. By reading this title you recognize and agree to take complete and total responsibility for yourself, your experience, and your actions.

Publisher's Cataloging-In-Publication Data
(Prepared by The Donohue Group, Inc.)

Names: Dunblazier, Tracee. | Penn, Michael J., illustrator.
Title: Master your inner world : embrace your power with joy / Tracee Dunblazier; illustrations: Michael J Penn.
Description: Baton Rouge, Louisiana; Los Angeles, California : GoTracee Publishing LLC, [2016] | Series: The Demon Slayer's handbook series | Includes bibliographical references.
Identifiers: LCCN 2016907522 | ISBN 978-0-9963907-4-3
Subjects: LCSH: Spiritualism. | Self-realization--Religious aspects. | Spiritual healing. | Negativism. | Emotions.
Classification: LCC BF1275.S44 D86 2016 | DDC 133.9--dc23

Printed in the United States of America

Dedication

This book is dedicated with tremendous gratitude to the courageous demon slayers who came before; to the slayers who continue to access, innovate, and express all that the Creator has given them; and to all slayers to come, whose ingenuity will transform this world as we know it, not just because they can but because they must. The journey out of darkness is rich with the obligation of love. An obligation we will all inevitably surrender to. Love is the way and the reward.

Acknowledgements

I've always considered myself lucky, to have what I need when I needed it, in such a magical way. Now, I recognize what I defined as luck was my awareness of the Creators offerings to me. The more I was willing to receive the more I was given. That was the gift of this book to me.

I'd like to thank God's offerings—my family, living and in spirit; the spiritual warriors with whom I have worked; my friends, support, and crew: Doreen, Margay, Lisa, Faith, Sammie, Kathleen, Tita, Jean Marie, Naomi, Jorge, Mariea, Kristine, Mike, Eric, Nelly, Kathleen T., Sara, Jennifer, Google, and Apothic Red—for the boundless humor and hilarity provided daily, the enormous support from long drives and conversations, meals together sharing stories, and the trust that was placed in me by sharing your resources on all levels.

May the blessings rain down on you like never before, and may your open heart receive them effortlessly.

Tracee Dunblazier

Contents

Part 4—Be Present

Foreword

Judging from the great number of requests for help in freeing individuals from demonic attack that we receive daily, Tracee Dunblazier is answering a need that those afflicted by negative entities are desperately seeking. In *Master Your Inner World: Embrace Your Power with Joy*, Tracee reveals a great number of methods ancient and modern, tribal and urban, that she has employed both to stand her ground in the face of personal demonic attack and that she has utilized to release others from the soul-devouring grasp of parasitic invaders. The book is filled with dramatic case histories. Tracee time and again demonstrates her familiarity with a vast number of spiritual practices and techniques. Written in a style that is personable and easy to read, we think that any reader who is in need of assistance of slaying one's personal demons—or who wishes to help others slay theirs—will find this book invaluable.

Brad and Sherry Steiger

Authors, *Real Miracles, Divine Intervention,*
and *Feats of Incredible Survival*

Preface

Fight the Devil and Win: One Demon at a Time

All of my experiences in this life have been connected to echoes of untapped pain from past centuries. Pain doesn't go away with time; it patiently waits until it can be exorcised and transformed into something different, something better.

Pain holds your soul together and follows you from incarnation to incarnation awaiting your attention. It is this process that cultivates compassion and opens your heart. As a spiritual empath, when the opportunity came for my heart to break open and let out some of that ancient pain, I took a deep breath, closed my eyes, and let my vocal cords take over.

It is my divine privilege to experience the healing of many incarnations of injustice within myself and to facilitate that same experience for others. I find that nothing strikes fear in people more than what they don't understand and can't control or (at the very least) can't find some humor in.

Fear and Courage

Fear and courage go hand in hand and both came in abundance for me. In fact, I've learned that you cannot have one without the other. When I think back on the many profound experiences of my spiritual journey within my life so far, the much larger picture becomes clear to me and seems so simple.

There has never been a time in this life that I have been confused about who I truly am. The one constant theme is courage that overtakes fear, clarity that commandeers confusion, and ugliness that always gives way to beauty. So in retrospect, my garden path of brick became golden right before my eyes. My life, and the main events that dotted it, no longer provoked self-pity but rather laughter from the irony.

The rhythm goes something like this: My father died when I was eleven, virginity raped from me at eighteen, moved to a New York City ghetto instead of going to college at Texas Christian University, and finally moving to Los Angeles and ending up with a career as a psychic. Trust me, I know how easy it is to judge.

For me, spirit is visibly palpable, but for others spirit is merely imagination, making healing very difficult. It is in this gap in perception where I started to understand why some people do not heal and how I needed to. Healing is a journey, not a judgement against you if you don't believe in what you can't see, or if you see things you just can't believe. I wrote this book to create the opportunity for all of us to expand our awareness and experience of spirit.

In the process of healing, our culture doesn't always begin at the origin of a life pattern. We often stick to the symptoms caused by the pattern, because we've been taught to fear what we are not familiar with.

I found that I couldn't heal completely on all levels without taking a look at the origins of fear. Understanding the function of fear—it is a tool to assist in staying alive, in keeping my body intact, and in keeping my spirit attached to my body in this reality—was vital. With this new understanding, I conceptualized what it would be like to begin to create the tools necessary to live and what the potential results might be, ultimately bringing me around to loving myself unconditionally, accepting others as they are, and being demon free.

It was prophesied by many that the decades proceeding the year 2012—the end of the Mayan calendar's 25,000-year cycle—would bring many trials and tribulations. The end times, they said, would lead us to a completely new world. The Bible talks about the final battles with the devil as being battles with principalities.

The tribulations of the Mayans and the battles in the Book of Revelation are symbols of what I recognized in this modern age as the struggle for *self*. I didn't need to prove my theory, whether it be that ghosts exist, that conspiracies are real, or that God and the devil do or do not exist. What I had to do was find the information that would create the space and allow me to heal mentally, emotionally, and spiritually but most of all, to understand the spirit, mind, body connection so that I could remain healthy. I found that my spiritual and emotional wellness supported or directly and immediately impacted my daily health.

Growing up, nobody wanted to talk about the difficult or profound stuff. Certainly, there weren't any books that could talk about demons, sex, death, and drugs. Those were all the experiences, fears, and imprints that I struggled with all before the age of eleven. One of the things I know is that when you're facing the devil head-on, or running for your life, fear is your friend—but not completely. Your fear will eventually turn on you.

Every day we carry images, energies, strategies, hopes, and dreams of times gone-by. These can take hold in the subtle bodies of our energy field and stay with us for lifetimes. Through my own spiritual journey I have relied on parts of myself, tools of my personality, people who have lived inside of me, and lifetimes I've lived before.

It doesn't matter how I describe them; they are all the elements of my wholeness that make me a unique expression of the divine. Through the *ripped from Tracee's headlines* stories and the exercises of realization that I've created in this work, it's my hope you will find breakthrough moments for your spirit and gain understanding that is relevant to knowing what makes you a unique expression of the Creator.

Writing this book has proven to be quite a challenge as I do not have a lot of memory, no doubt a byproduct of doing this work for as many years as I have. As an empath, I mostly have a catch and release policy; when working with clients, I listen and then grieve their experiences so that I don't retain them for any length of time.

Although I have access to everything I've experienced intuitively, I really just don't remember some things. Doing shamanic work requires that I set aside myself for a little while and carry the spirit of someone else. There have been times when I have felt the grief of thousands. I believe that I am able to work as a spiritual empath because I accept my immense power as a spiritual being while recognizing that I am human and need specific things in order to recover from my spiritual and emotional journeys.

Having said all of that, this book is written without the benefit of notes providing the exact names, dates, and places. What I do have is the spiritual essence, emotional memory, and divine message of each and every experience that I have ever had, whether it is mine or someone else's.

Don't get me wrong: some things I remember as if it were five minutes ago, but I have decided to write the anecdotes commemorated here from the perspective of their purpose and perceived facts rather than a biographical account of each person's story. All of the names and defining details of each story have been changed to preserve any right to privacy, and what is left is the spiritual meaning and teaching of the anecdote. One of the things I have recognized over the years is that people truly hear first what they believe, and secondly, maybe they hear the facts. So it is my hope that you find interest in these stories and see some of yourself within them.

You may read each volume of the series in any order. Each part in a volume contains a parable or story from my personal spiritual history of a spirit guide or past life. The five parables of *Master Your Inner World: Embrace Your Power with Joy* are the stories of the spirit guides that have worked with me in this lifetime and for some over many lifetimes. A spirit guide is a being who's in spirit and a mentor here to be of service to you for a lifetime or through specific experiences and transitions in your life. They've been my teachers and companions through the darkness and into the light. They stood by me in every battle, showing me how to fight the devil and win.

The five parables of *Heal Your Soul History: Activate the True Power of Your Shadow* are of actual, past lifetimes that my spirit has lived; and I have relived them in this lifetime by processing out the emotional memory that I carried. In telling their story, it was important for me to be historically accurate about the history and social mores of the times, but unnecessary to prove the existence of the specific people.

The purpose of telling these stories is to give them all the voice of justice and truth that they all suffered so greatly to receive. All of the details of spiritual sentiment and experiences were channeled from each of the main characters in each story while the names and specific details were inspired by them but given by me for symbolic purposes. Dreams, visions, and events triggered the past memories, and each illustration was created from how each of them presented to me.

Please don't be thrown by the graphic nature of the parables and stories. I understand that not everyone has a life as traumatic as the ones I have depicted, but in fact some do. It will be important to call on the meaning and understanding of each spiritual dynamic inherent in each story, and figure out how it applies to you. There is no reality, only perception. I write this book as an opportunity for you—not to take my truth as your own, but to allow my truth to light up yours and reflect back all that the Creator has given you, to ease your suffering, and to help you experience deep and complete spiritual healing, knowing that when the spirit heals all other levels will follow.

In this book you may find that I use a word that traditionally carries a particular meaning, but I have used it with a different understanding or connotation. My goal here is not to rewrite the English language, but to do my best to convey the depth of these ideas in the simplest way possible, while having reverence for the wordsmiths who have come before me.

It is my intrinsic belief that people are always smarter and wiser and less fearful than they act like they are. This belief has made me always dig deeper within myself and look further into others for the thumping of the eternal heart.

When you know what I know, you can't be a bigot or a racist, a victim or a perpetrator; you can't believe that there is only one path to the Creator, or that death is real.

Most of all, I know we are all of the same essence and that you know what I know somewhere hidden in the secret of your past, present, and future. Somewhere deep within yourself lies the mystery of *wyrd*.[1] You can only be a part of all that is.

---

1   Fate or destiny

Introduction

A Matter of Spirit

No matter the state of darkness or light, everything has a purpose; those who seek to understand this purpose will find an easy justice. Whether or not you believe in demons, entities, ghosts, earth-bound spirits, depression, mental illness, or insanity, they are a daily truth for some and will touch all in some way during their lifetime. This is an arena in life where ignorance is not bliss—it's just ignorance. The remedy here is knowledge all the way around, to know yourself, to know truth, and to act with compassion.

One question that I believe deep down we all want to know is how can we as individuals take responsibility and be empowered in our part of the world dynamic?

The answer to this question is a matter of spirit. It is common to make the assumption that spiritual matters are religious matters. They are not one and the same. Religion is the spiritual ritual that aligns us with our spirit and our relationship with the Creator; it is not the relationship itself.

In order for all of us to progress, we must acknowledge ourselves as energetic/ spiritual beings. It is unnecessary that we be religious but imperative that we be spiritual. We must acknowledge that our physical body is very dense energy. As the frequency rises the energy patterns become faster and more subtle but not less powerful.

Our energy body, emotions, and thoughts are all forms of this *less dense* matter. All of these forms of matter are propelled by the faster frequencies of energy that preceded them. So when you want to heal completely, you must go to where the energy pattern started the formation of matter in its most subtle, spiritual form.

In the modern world, we don't care what you believe, or what you call your beliefs. We just require that you are willing to give a name to your personal struggle. Here, the devil is all the expressions of illusion that exist, from imagination to the formation of constructs and demons.

The devil's only goal is to exist, and its role in this book is that of the all-pervasive, multipurpose antagonist.

Every person's experience of the devil is different, and I believe that the more we all understand each other's experience, the less we will have the need to stay in judgment or impose our ways onto others. The truth in our lives reveals the paths we will take on our journey of perception; truth is the central theme of our spiritual development. It is the destination everyone seeks. It has many faces and stages, and can be loving and kind, or harsh and formidable. Our perception of truth is the only true adversary.

Exploring the five basic levels of perception—physical, etheric, emotional, mental, and causal—is very important because each has a very specific point of reference. This book is about people experiencing all their many parts. It is about witnessing, persevering, enduring, and believing in our ability to heal completely and fully on all levels.

In essence, it is about recognizing our wholeness.

Healing can at times be a progression and at other times may appear to be instantaneous. Learning to accept healing starts with a willingness to accept the illusions we carry about ourselves and others, whether they be ancient or newly born. Accepting your fear, accepting your love, accepting your desire for the information that your illusions bring here and now—all this allows your illusions to be a part of the natural world.

The natural world is the place where all things end or truly begin. The natural world has the final say as to when and how any thought, idea, or concept becomes physically manifest. Spirit, energy, and creativity are all manifestations of our oneness, the Creator, and they eventually become atoms and molecules.

The parts of our spiritual world that will become manifest in our physical world are the places we put our focus. In between your perception of the worlds of spirit and matter, there is a gap where all energy flows. Whatever you believe fills the gap. Whatever you fear fills the gap. Whatever you love fills the gap. This is our path to recognize and honor the gap. Good, bad, or indifferent, all things are sacred.

Accepting where you are today gives you power, the ability to make another decision. If you are fearful of making a decision, accepting that fear as a part of your reality can place you in a position to embrace that fear. If you embrace your fear of committing to an idea, then you are able to access, modify, or innovate what you need in order to create change.

Instead of doing nothing, tell yourself: *Just for today, I will use discipline. Just for today, I will commit to the task at hand. If I want to change my mind tomorrow I can, but just for today I will commit.*

Once you have modified your experience in any way, the dynamic changes. Changing the dynamic every day leads to thought innovation, and as thought innovation sets in, the option for fear has changed completely. This book will address some of the historical belief systems that exist about the human struggle; the spiritual process of their origins, including mental illness, demons, addiction, and sexuality; and how negative thinking is the Creator's message to you in dark times.

The spiritual process is the series of steps each of us must have gone through, are going through, or will go through, in order first to understand the purpose of the spiritual patterns we have been encoded with, and secondly to begin integrating the results of that understanding into our wholeness.

As an empath, it is my expertise to live in the world of illusion and delusion and to master the recognition of the creation of the physical world by witnessing the entire process of emotional perception.

Brain research now shows that perception is a fundamental building block of decision-making. Emotions such as anger, grief, humiliation, disappointment, and confusion are some of the dynamics that will be looked at, understanding that each emotion can be interpreted based on the layer of energy that one focuses through, and that each emotion can have several meanings.

> Did you know that in the Mandarin language, one word can have several meanings? The word ma, for example, has four different meanings based on the intonation that you use to pronounce the word: one intonation means mother and another intonation means dog...There is a lot of room for error here, as there is with the emotional perception of others.

What something means to me is based on the lens that I am looking through. If you don't know or understand my lens, then you don't know my meaning. Through the reinterpretation of difficult feelings, you will begin to innovate your own thoughts, which will allow you to be more intuitive when it comes to understanding others.

Master Your Inner World: Embrace Your Power with Joy also speaks about fear, how you feel when you experience fear, and that through naming the fear gives you a definitive way to address it so that it is changed forever.

Planetary change requires us to shift on all levels: physically, energetically, emotionally, mentally, and spiritually. Through global warming, fracking, and other disruptions caused by humanity, we experience earthquakes, tsunamis, and other natural events on our planet. Humanity *en masse* experiences these same changes internally. In the natural rhythm of this spiritual integration, an identifiable process occurs. When we can recognize our place in this process we are better able to navigate our evolution through understanding ourselves.

An old adage, *water seeks its own level,* describes the spiritual concept of the lowest common denominator. Every person has a lowest common denominator, the part of themselves that is of the densest frequency, such as feelings of lack, hate, grief, inferiority, etc. This lowest common denominator can't spiritually evolve until the self has gone through a process of spiritual evolution. And, the lens in which he looks through has been transformed or raised up to another, more expansive, form of seeing and experiencing life. The lowest common denominator can be found in all layers of the mind, body, and spirit.

Choice is the first tool to master. It begins with the concept that the consciousness of every human being is made of a *high self, middle self,* and *low self.* In this model, the higher self is the highest frequency we have access to. The middle self is the cognizant mind while the low self is all of the energy that is contained in our spirit—or as I refer to it, *the gap.*

When the conscious mind decides to do something, it makes its request to the higher self. Prior to success, all the information in the spirit is scanned to determine what obstacles exist to the manifestation of the idea. All focus will then move to the lowest common denominator of the energy or the most formidable obstacle. Discerning what beliefs or ideologies can stay and support the emerging idea, or which ones need to be recycled.

If we have beliefs that won't allow for the manifestation of our desire, then our choices are likely to match our beliefs and not our desires. We now know what belief systems we have in place that are not in alignment with what we want, and we can choose to give them up and adopt new ones that match our goals.

Many spiritual philosophies hold a concept known as the *holy death*, which refers to a death or completion of the spirit. When death occurs in any situation, it marks the end of one dynamic and the beginning of a new one. If we acknowledge that all things are created of spirit, then spirit would be the place to go to make changes to those creations.

What it takes to heal

Healing requires a relentless desire to heal, unequivocal commitment and devotion to the process, and a complete trust in the deepest parts of yourself for having created the conflict (on a spiritual level) in the first place. It is only through brutal honesty—and a few laughs—that we can heal ourselves and this planet. I hope that this book will be the beginning of that process for others as it has been for me.

Everyone has his or her own ghosts of events passed, of people wronged, of the irrevocable choices made by you or affecting you. No matter how these energies present themselves, or the paradigm with which you look at them, they are there and can be reconciled in some way. You do not have to continue to live with them. They can be transformed and healed when you recognize their purpose. This book, while truthful, is not designed to be *the* truth, but to mirror the reader's truth back to them. The sections of each chapter are connected with one another in terms of meaning and understanding, but the logic is not exact and linear.

Whether or not the concept of past lives is a part of your belief system is irrelevant here; what is true is that we all carry with us imprints of spiritual knowledge that, when processed, awaken in us a truth, wisdom, and understanding about ourselves.

These imprints of spiritual knowledge convey to us a dynamic that both no longer serves us and includes the way out of the old dynamic, all in one package. These imprints are called the Akashic records, our soul's personal lineage of how we know all that we know. The Akashic records oftentimes offer us the opportunity to grieve what was left behind, and—through the action of grief—create space in the brain to affirm a new dynamic all the way down to the biochemical level.

Each chapter includes several sections: *The Slayer's Weapons, The Slayer's Path, The Slayer's Motto, The Slayer's Pact,* and *The Slayer's Altar* (or *ritual*).

- *The Slayer's Weapons* are positive or negative dynamics that we all experience, such as joy or self-pity. It is through these dynamics that the Slayer is able to witness herself and others and learn about her deepest spiritual expression, transforming her patterns and environment.

- *The Slayer's Path* gives a concept that helps the slayer align with their truth during the particular phase of development that the Slayer may be experiencing.

- *The Slayer's Motto* is a tagline or affirmation that a slayer can repeat over and over again to remind himself of his chosen path.

- *The Slayer's Pact* is a unifying idea that all slayers commit to on their journey.

- And finally, *the Slayer's Altar* or *Ritual* is the physical world completion that cements the slayer's commitment to her or his desire to overcome any deeply rooted pervasive energy and then to heal on every level.

The information in the chapters will educate you about demons and all the spiritual dynamics that we humans can be affected by. You will learn things like who and what demons are, where they live, how they were created, and how and why they function as they do.

You will also be illuminated as to what you already have, and what you need to have, in order to commence victory over every one of them. You will gain an understanding of your personal spiritual tools that you've brought into this life and the dynamics within you that are being healed.

The anecdotes in this book are inspired by real life accounts but are in no way accurate to anyone's exact experience. I've created them to illustrate in a defined way the specific spiritual dynamics that I believe are the most valuable and necessary for this teaching.

Again, the elements of the book are interactive and can include information that connects with any of the parables and stories. The purpose of this design is for you the reader to be able to access your own personal stories and truths through the process of working through this book.

Finally, each chapter is my personal story, containing some of the events, past-life visions, and spiritual experiences that illuminated my soul guides and stories. I have always been empathic, psychic, and fully aware of my spiritual knowledge, even from as early as my days in the crib. I don't think I am unique in this experience, and I believe that many of our world citizens today are opening up to their own personal knowledge or are born with the empathetic awareness of their gifts, or *tools* as I prefer to call them.

This book offers strategies for balancing life's traumas and dares us to have the audacity to laugh and see the world through someone else's eyes. A spiritual perspective coupled with real-life accounts, mixed with how-tos and how-not-tos, will be helpful to those who are willing to help themselves.

In our culture today there is a lot of focus on all that we have lost and are losing. As I contemplated it, we're bringing light to even darker and denser places in our spirits and in our world.

It is my hope that everyone within the sound of my voice will seek their truth and that through this book all readers will embrace and face their demons whatever they may be, gaining a deeper understanding of themselves, others, and the way the universe works. Finally, I hope that you will know that grief and suffering are simply a part of the spiritual process of being beautiful and peaceful, and that peace is inevitable for everyone who makes the effort.

Please feel free to work with this book however you are guided to. Read it in order, out of order, only parts of it, or in whatever way you need in order to metabolize the right information at the right time.

And if you've been led to this book, then without a doubt it has something for you or for someone you know. So go forth and conquer.

PART 1
Play on Your Field

Demons will always find you—never go to them

The Slayer's Weapons:

Determination, Leadership, Levity, Trust, Awareness

The Story of NGUVU JABARI: Never Lose

The forest was rich that morning with silence. It was as if all the creatures, big and small, knew something was coming. It had been blowing in the wind off the great water for days now.

Nguvu Jabari had taken his people deep into the forest past a cliff that held the perfect hiding place. From the water, it looked like a steep, jagged rock, formidable and unforgiving. No one would ever go there willingly. On the other side of it, down in the rock, was a crevice that threaded along the north wall in a gentle way, down to the floor. There was even a waterfall leading to a much larger pool underground. The space was almost perfectly round and could hold upwards of one hundred people comfortably. Now there were only about seventy-nine left in the tribe and two had stayed behind: Nguvu and his apprentice. Someone would have to take over when he was gone. That was the plan.

Nguvu Jabari was the chief and spiritual leader of his tribe, one of the original seeds of the planet; he never seemed to age. Standing 6'8", Nguvu was a giant of a man with strong, forthright muscles and piercing black eyes. So strong and powerful were the emanations from his black eyes, that most who knew him weren't completely comfortable in meeting his gaze. That's where his power came from: the spirit that flowed through his eyes.

In his locks were recorded the path of lifetimes of survival, triumph, and leadership. The locks were laced with knuckles and teeth along with colorful beads and whittled sticks. Each one of them told the story of a journey he had taken on someone's behalf, a battle won, or a request from his god. He had rich brown skin that was slightly scarred and riddled with the wear and tear of his obligations. His presence was massive, an event in its own right. His feet and spear were large enough to carry his spirit; he had flanks like a stallion that carried the rest. Simply adorned, a piece of animal skin was tied around his middle. Nguvu Jabari remembered who he was and he knew he could never lose. It was the most powerful tool he possessed. There is never loss—only surrender.

There was still much to do. Nguvu Jabari had many friends in the forest, for he could speak with all creatures. He had been sending out his plea for help for four days now. It wasn't just any ordinary assistance that he needed. It was blood. Finally the answer to his request arrived.

It was mating season. One of the gorillas had come of age and had tried to take his place in a troop on the other side of the forest; to the young gorilla's dismay, he was badly injured. There was a lot of blood. The birds brokered a deal that Nguvu Jabari would save him, if he could have some of his blood. It was done. The gorilla bled into the ground all around a sacred space with a large, flat, beveled rock. Nguvu had chosen this place, about five hundred yards up from the beach in a little clearing. They positioned the gorilla so the rock could be sufficiently covered with blood as well while Nguvu stitched him up.

The time was approaching for the arrival, and they needed to get the gorilla strong enough to travel on his own, at least a few miles without a trace. They fed him, washed him, and gave him a special plant concoction that would give him the strength to move immediately. The apprentice added enough water to double the apparent amount of blood, and the plan was now in motion. They were all lucky that day.

Now it was the eve before the arrival. The apprentice helped build the ceremonial pyre. He had been hunting for dry wood for days so that there would be an enormous amount of ash left behind. The perfect mix of ash and sand was what they needed. The entire forest could see the smoke. Nguvu Jabari sat in stillness watching the continual flames. All night long there was a low buzz in the air, a sort of dismal excitement. His heart and adrenaline were even in their movement. He sat in the fullness of his spirit and in oneness with his Universe.

Know that there is never loss, but only acceptance of what is, and to know your power within it—for all things move in a great circle, never ending.

Nguvu Jabari

It was time to pull back his forces from his people and transfer the love and energy of his obligation to his apprentice. His apprentice was a stealthily wise man for his young age. Nguvu noticed that from very early on this young one could look him straight in the eye without hesitation, and Nguvu knew that he was the one to carry on his legacy. Nguvu had no children and yet everyone descended from him.

"You see, legacy is not by blood or ancestry but by spiritual path," he would always say.

As the time came he stood with his apprentice and said, "It is now time to remember who you are. Not your belief about me nor the sacrifices I am making and what that means for you, but to remember the beginning seed of your heart; to absolutely know your spirit, who up until this day has only followed you. Now you must honor and follow it, the seed of the Creator inside of you, and take your place in your Universe. Know that there is never loss, but only acceptance of what is, and know your power within it. For all things move in a great circle, never ending. Go, and take care of our people."

There was enough wood to burn for at least four more hours, but it would all be over long before then. Nguvu could see the sails of the ship on the horizon.

The spot he had chosen for the bloody rock was up an easy path from the water. He did not want to make it too complicated for them, as their expectations were low already. He had taken some of the blood and covered his face and body with it. The fire was still burning strong, and there was ash enough for eighty bodies. He now sat on the sturdy rock waiting.

Just as dawn was breaking he heard rustling on the path. In his mind's eye he saw what it really was: it was large and grizzly, almost as if it had no skin. The low-lit, red eyes took up most of its thorny face, except for the several rows of teeth that resembled wooden spikes. Its thumping tail made the ground shake from its stupidity and gluttonous anticipation. It traveled with a group of about five spindly men.

They tried to keep their voices down, but they couldn't contain their wrathful, whispering glee. They chattered on in insincere gratitude about how effortless the savages had made it for them. They traveled down the easy path lead by it, the one with the red eyes and gnashing teeth. Quickly, they arrived upon Nguvu Jabari, who was sitting jovially covered in blood with his eyes closed. They were a bit confused.

Nguvu opened his eyes and said, "I have been waiting for you. I am all you will need and all you will get." As he laughed, he said, "I have killed the rest."

Nguvu Jabari, the Force of God

Nguvu Jabari is a tribal leader and shaman, and his name means *the strength or force of God* in Swahili. Nguvu is many things: a member of my spiritual lineage, a spirit guide, an aspect of myself. His essence has been with me for as long as I can remember, guiding and protecting me—at times from others and at times from myself. His presence gives new meaning to gratitude, for how can you appropriately be thankful to the essence of the origin of all that you are. It's like being thankful to H_2O, O_2, and salt.

The Slayer's Path: Be Yourself and Slay

All of us, in some way, are demon slayers, but there are definitely two kinds of slayers: those who follow the path of the slayer for a time and those who follow the path of the slayer for a lifetime. No matter which one you are, the rules of the game are the same.

Being or becoming a slayer is a special phase of spiritual development in which you cultivate very specific skills that you sustain and use over an entire lifetime. A temporary slayer, though requiring the same skills as those used by a lifetime slayer, uses her abilities only for a time, often in situational and conditional contexts. After the time has passed, she becomes a *watcher*. This person will always have the awareness and skills that were developed, but she will use the knowledge in silence holding the secrets of those she crosses paths with. She won't necessarily have a life where those skills will be in constant demand.

Unlike a watcher a slayer intervenes in some way. Both roles are vital for communities in spiritual transformation. A watcher holds the secrets for the people being transformed, while a slayer always knows the best method of approach, whether it is one of confrontation or submission. Make no mistake about it: being on the slayer's path can be dangerous and deserves your undivided attention and respect. Being on high alert is a natural state for a demon slayer, who has very special needs for nourishment and care.

Demons 101

You have the power

This is the first thing you need to know about demons: you have all the power. Don't forget that. *You* have *all* the power. Demons don't want you to know that. Now that you know that, we can move forward.

So many people have such fear of demons. Given their history, I can understand why. However, you can only fear something as long as you don't understand it. I'd like to demystify it for you. Don't worry if you've heard that just hearing about demons will call them to you. The truth is some people already have an awareness of them in some way, or will in the future, and some won't ever. If you've decided to read this chapter or buy this book, then you probably already have the vision and some understanding or will need it in your future. All you will get from reading this is empowerment. If you don't know in your heart that you have all the power, then you are not ready and should consider moving on to another chapter.

Again, the first thing to know about dealing with actual creepy entities from the underworld is that they are in *your* world; you are not in theirs. They need an invitation and a source of energy to be here. Now let me break down the basics.

> The idea is that humans or other beings are not inherently evil, but they can adopt, and be harmed by, the spirit of sin.

The beginning

Many people think that it is only Christianity, Islam, and Judaism that have a belief in demons, but almost every religion has deep within its texts, stories of demonic beings and their minions. The concept of a demon isn't something that is conjured simply in order to explain evil; the concept of a demon comes from the understanding that energy is fluid and can be endowed with human emotion. The idea is that humans or other beings are not inherently evil, but they can adopt, and be harmed by, the spirit of sin.

Take, for example, the emotion of anger. Anger vibrates at a much lower rate than, say, irritation or frustration. The use of prayer to avert evil is

9

based on the idea that prayer helps us refuse the temptation of possession by the spirit of anger; that we don't allow ourselves to be given over to anger, to target someone else with anger, or to create karma based on our anger.

You can feel and express anger without pointing it at someone. Feeling the anger is a temptation; sin would be using that emotion to hurt yourself or someone else. Recognize that feeling anger is evidence of unprocessed trauma or pain, an energy that you've repressed, or overlooking your own needs. When you express your energy without harming another, you are no longer vulnerable to any other entity that may seek to capitalize on your unexpressed energy.

The Slayer's Path: **Be Yourself and Slay**

The starter demon

In truth, the emotion of anger has a very important job, and specific role, within your spiritual dynamics. Anger is the emotion that elevates or expands your belief or recognition of the Creator. Anger transitions you from your image of the Creator to what or who the Creator truly is. So when you target someone or something with your anger, you keep yourself from expanding your image of the Creator and the truth.

Your heart and throat actually open to joy and love when you express anger. However, when you pinpoint your anger, you repress and focus it on yourself or your target. Your target is the object of your anger but not necessarily what you are mad about at all. Targeting is a way of seeking understanding through blame. When you choose someone to be at fault, you naturally and spiritually feel guilt. (Guilt is the unconscious mind saying you are overlooking your heart and your needs.) Even if a situation appears to be someone's fault, if you were to actually trace the situation back to every decision that was made, to the people and thought-forms that influenced it, then you would find a thousand hands contributing to the situation and that no one specifically is at fault.

Often, when something bad happens, people don't let themselves be sad and cry. Crying allows you to eventually reflect on what happened and why, ultimately leading you to the information you need to find forgiveness for yourself and the others involved. Grief is the process. Processing emotion means that you take the energy and change its form from one vibration to another.

Go back millions of years to a time we don't really know a lot about. Back to, say, the caveman days when the spiritual energy on the planet was much denser, and we had yet to cultivate a body or mind that could process the spiritual understanding of the Creator. That gift was held only by a few. The population was slim by today's standards. Now imagine you are a man living in a cave with your mate and small baby. You arise one morning, go out of the cave to greet the sun and smell the morning dew, and who should be there to meet you but a saber-toothed tiger. The huge beast catches you off guard, nips you up into its jaws, and begins to run.

"Aaah!"

From your mouth, the energy and adrenaline of profound fear and fury are released as you fight for life. *Devastated* and *terrified* don't begin to come close to your feelings as you slowly (so it seems) come to an abrupt, grievous demise.

Whew, just thinking about it—the agony of the powerlessness you must have felt—makes me sad.

Now, imagine two things about this scenario: the energy of fear, fury, and powerlessness that the caveman screamed out just before his abrupt death and his bodiless spirit. The profundity of his emotion has gone unexpressed—the confusion, disorientation, and disbelief as he sits by his body, but not in it.

Now what? he must be thinking.

His fearful, disgruntled, and possibly angry spirit roams the area as it settles into what has happened to him. Now he must feed on energy where he finds it. Desperate to communicate with his wife and his precious baby, all he does is scare them. In his frustration, the anger and fear turn to fury, resentment, and rage.

This bodiless spirit is not able to grieve his loss because the anger doesn't allow for access to what he really wants: to say goodbye to his wife and son and to share his love with them. He roams the earth for what is his eternity, not finding help or salvation. It is now the twentieth century. His hollow rage has taken form, not physically but as a thick, formidable essence of rage and bitterness. It has grown horns and a tail and now only seeks the chaos and pleasure of creating havoc and scaring the bejesus out of some poor unsuspecting schmuck in his path. There is no longer the appearance of love or compassion, only annihilation.

This is just a single example of how energy takes form.

> A demon has never incarnated in the physical realm. A demon has never been formed in matter. It is a creation that lives in its own dimension or vibration of energy.

To break it down a little more, initially, when our caveman dies, we call him *discarnate*. His spirit is thrust from his body, but because of the trauma is not in a spiritual vibration sufficient for ascension to the *oversoul*, a term that acknowledges the spiritual connection and unity of all things. So, he becomes a spirit roaming without a body. Then there is the element of fear and rage that is present within his spirit. In this scenario, our caveman is unable to separate from the spirit of fear and rage, and therefore he feeds it.

Let's suppose at some point in the distant future the spirit of the man is ready to be ascended back to his oversoul. He will first need to be delivered from the spirit of fear and rage. If both of these spiritual elements stay intact for years, decades, or perhaps centuries, then both will gain power, energy, and essence as they are fed by the energies in their environments and manifest lives in their own spiritual dimension. The difference between the spirit of the man and the spirit of fear and rage is that the discarnate human spirit eventually has an oversoul to go to; whereas the energy of the fear and rage, over time and with the feeding of the collective, can become a demon. A demon has never incarnated in the physical realm. A demon has never been formed in matter. It is a creation that lives in its own dimension or vibration of energy. That's why a demon must have our invitation in order to connect to us.

Your fitness in dealing with demonic intrusion varies at any given time, but you are always anointed with the necessary skills, discipline (even though it may be uncultivated), and resources to secure your deliverance.

The Slayer's Motto: Take Authority

Demons are personal

We are born into our own personal microcosm of the macrocosm; our spirit is born into our body into the world. Likewise, our demons are born of this journey as well, and people often carry demons along down the ancestral line, until they can be metabolized and transformed into acceptance, forgiveness, and healing.

So, yes, if you have demons they are personal to you. If you are around others who are afflicted, then at some point you have also been afflicted. Your fitness in dealing with demonic intrusion varies at any given time, but you are always anointed with the necessary skills, discipline (even though it may be uncultivated), and resources to secure your deliverance.

That is for certain.

Our souls are ancient and we are all imprinted with what are called Akashic records, our personal software that tells us who we are. The imprints of many life stories are contained in these records, things our souls have experienced and discovered, as well as things that we fear and have yet to overcome. Whether or not you believe in the concept of having lived before in another time, you must recognize that the information about who you are is contained in your spirit.

Now, there are definitely some folk who really don't have a lot of complexity to them at all, and their focuses in life appear to be simple and contained. Keep in mind that there are no beginners—or *new souls* as some call them—on this journey, only old souls with new hardware. We can never lose the history and wisdom we gain; we can only move our focus away from that history and wisdom.

People come into this world with a purpose and the appropriate beliefs and ideologies to fulfill it. To truly know another person means to be able to access, acknowledge, and accept their purpose and all the imprints that come with it. You can't judge a person based on your own perception unless you are able to completely empathize and experience their situation from their point of view. For the most part, when it appears that you are judging another, you are only making an assessment of yourself on some level.

For example, you know how when you have a bad breakup things are left unsaid, and then you run into them somewhere and all of those repressed feelings come flooding back? Well, whether or not you express them, the feelings are there waiting to be expressed. Depending on how long you wait, those feelings attract more energy and experiences that resonate with them, until they finally are too heavy not to express or resolve. Imagine the bitterness that can be cultivated through a lifetime of failed or disappointing relationships, and what happens to that energy when the person dies unresolved in it. Where does that energy go and what does it look like?

The Slayer's Motto: **Take Authority**

Now, let's say somewhere along your soul's continuum you were literally scared to death, and that fear and abrupt demise was left unprocessed by your soul. What might that energy have manifested five thousand years later? Have you ever had a chronic illness? Were you born with a scar or birthmark? Have you ever had dreams or night terrors that don't align with your life experiences? Or maybe you have feelings about a different culture even though you have no conscious experience with it? These are all ways that your soul communicates with you via the imprints that you carry. They are all part of the many clues to your personal mystery just waiting to be investigated.

The good news is that when you embrace the process of discovery, your path becomes fun, exhilarating, and—at times—awe-inspiring. These are all sentiments that help you overcome the illusion of difficulty, confusion, or fear, illusions that inevitably play a profound role in the process of illumination as well.

Can you be afflicted by someone else's demon?

Yes and no. Let me repeat: if you are connected in any way to acknowledging this kind of energy, then you are or have been afflicted yourself. Judgment here is superfluous. If you are in fear of, or strongly resistant to, this information then you are connected in an unconscious way as opposed to a conscious way. It will ultimately prove unhelpful to get angry and run from or abandon a relationship or situation that you may find yourself in because *the other person* happens to be afflicted.

However, not for nothing, this happens a lot and is a completely common response to have. It is a response to the recognition of a bit of our own story. We tend to fight deeply against or resist the information that has yet to become a part of our cognizant understanding of ourselves.

How I Became a Demon Slayer

Determination

Some of my oldest memories were of demon battle. I was a happy child yet plagued with otherworldly critters. Many nights I tossed and turned, sleepless and fearful. I usually went to bed with the closet light on, but always the dreams would come.

Sometimes it wasn't just dreams; it was the heavy hitters. One night I awoke in the middle of a gasp for air. I couldn't breathe. Something large, creepy, and four-legged was sitting on my chest. It didn't have a real body, but it was as heavy and real as it gets. I opened my eyes and caught a glimpse then immediately began reciting the Lord's Prayer. I must have been between four and six years old. At that point, I hadn't fully learned the Lord's Prayer or spent much time in church that I can remember.

I was baptized in a Methodist church as a baby, but that was about it. We weren't really a church-going family except for Christmas Eve. We always went to church on Christmas Eve. I have a great love for churches, so I made it my mission to go as often as possible with whoever would take me. The denomination didn't matter. I went to First Congregational, Burian Baptist, Queen of Angels, and a synagogue with various friends and relatives. When I was old enough, I went to Heights Christian on my own and even played Delilah in the "Holiday Parables."

> The good news is that when you embrace the process of discovery, your path becomes fun, exhilarating, and—at times—awe-inspiring.

Since I was a child, I could always see the nature of people and whether or not they had *company*—demons or other attachments. I call all these spiritual entities *critters* as a general term for the collective. I could look at them and see whether they had a good intent or bad. At the time, I thought it was the person, instead of the critter, with the bad intention. I understand differently now.

This wasn't anything I ever told anyone about; it was just a little secret I kept. I was about eight or nine years old, and as my nighttime's were getting scarier, I decided to take up with the Baptists. The Baptists were always so friendly, and somehow I knew they were good demon slayers. My childhood friend Lisa and her family went every Sunday. I don't remember how long I went or much of what we did except for once.

Madeleine was the lady who taught Bible study to the little children. One day she asked to speak with me and pulled me aside into a little room. She could see how distraught I was, and asked if I was okay. I told her that I knew my dad was sick.

She asked, "With what?"

I said I didn't know. The truth was that my parents didn't know, because he hadn't been diagnosed yet. All they knew at the time was that his cholesterol was a little high and that he needed to change his diet. He started eating granola and nonfat milk, and all seemed to be right with the world. But in fact, he had cancer of the kidneys that would go undiagnosed and eventually metastasize to the liver and pancreas and then take his life in about two or three years.

Madeleine asked me if I had asked Jesus into my heart, or if I would like to. She said it would help me. I don't know what I thought. But I was told that if I became a born-again Christian, then it would save my father's atheist soul. She asked me to get on my knees, fold my hands, tell Jesus whatever I wanted, and ask him into my heart. All of a sudden I felt this enormous white light enter my head and open my heart. At least I have words for it now. Then I just collapsed and wept.

She explained to me that if I was with Jesus, then all of my family would be saved as well. I felt extraordinary relief. My father was a dynamic and loving person who was always in service to others, so I couldn't really take any chances and needed to cover my bases. I walked out of the room with the power of the sword that day and never looked back.

I knew little about religion—at least from this life. But many Protestant, Catholic, Buddhist, and Jewish rituals seemed familiar, as if they were ingrained in my spirit already. I seemed to have a lot of actual memory, like knowing the Lord's Prayer in a way that could have only been achieved by years of repetition—and we didn't do repetition in my family.

The only thing about Christianity that troubled me from that very early age was the hypocrisy that I witnessed in people who spent a lot of time at church and the apparent contradictions within the Bible. I have a great love for all religions and the powerful mechanisms they offer to all spiritualists. I have a deep reverence for Jesus as well as all of the ascended masters who have graced our planet with their love, knowledge, and mastery.

Before we move on, I think it important that you know where I stand. I don't believe that any one is exclusively right; I believe that all ascended masters represent a function of enlightenment within the spiritual process as interpreted by human beings. Spiritual texts must be read through the lens of your heart, not your head, and all spiritual texts seek to explain the profound phenomena of the path to the Creator through the understanding of how our universe works through spirit, mind, and body. The God that I know adorns all hearts.

> Spiritual texts must be read through the lens of your heart, not your head, and all spiritual texts seek to explain the profound phenomena of the path to the Creator through the understanding of how our Universe works, through spirit, mind, and body.

Finding Acceptance in Connection

The robertson apartments

I spent about ten years being an overseer for an apartment complex in Los Angeles. By *overseer*, I mean property manager, but for me, it was

17

never really the property I managed—it was the space within and around this property and those it attracted to it. It truly is a magical place of transformation. I'd lived there for five years when I got the *call*, meaning the spiritual compulsion to be the fiduciary for this place of spiritual transformation and those it transformed.

I was called to live there about a month after the big Los Angeles earthquake in 1994. The property is situated on the cusp of Los Angeles proper. Back in the 1930s, before the Interstate 10 freeway, the Robertson Apartments were a quaint, little set of wood-built bungalows with a little sandwich shop on the property. Twentieth Century Fox Studios utilized it as a temporary lodging for employees.

In the 1950s, half of the property was taken over by the government claiming eminent domain, and the I-10 freeway was built straight through the complex, completely changing its size and structure. I believe this changed the energetic makeup of the complex forever. Having your land stolen...old story, I know.

In order to replace the units lost to eminent domain, a two-level apartment building was built in the back of the remaining set of twenty bungalows, and over the years a unique dynamic was set up. There seemed to be a caste system between the folks in the bungalows and the folks in the building. When I became the on-site manager, the administrative management would regularly call the people living in the building animals, and many of the people living in the building would refer to the bungalows as Beverly Hills. It was a fascinating phenomenon that always piqued my curiosity and saddened me at the same time. The truth of it was there were a few drug addicts, artists, musicians, and others with non-traditional life styles. I think the drug of choice for the acting manager when I moved in was meth, and heroin seemed to be popular for a few, but by the time I became manager there were only a few alcoholics left—some who in my tenure got sober.

I knew this land held special secrets. I was first attracted to the place because the earthquake had crushed the entire freeway just yards away from the building, yet no damage or harm came to it during the quake. I had several friends living there and not one of them had anything break, not even a glass. I tell you, the place was mystical.

> It was a low place steeped in so much of everything: joy, hate, fear, degradation, creativity, love, conflict, addiction, rage, and struggle. It was rich in all the things that make life good, bad, and savory.

The second thing that intrigued me was that the first three times I drove there to visit, I missed the place and drove past it. It was almost invisible. To make a long story short, I moved in with a roommate initially for nine months and then almost a year later returned for the duration of almost twenty years.

At that time, the Robertson Apartments already had the reputation of being LA's punk rock haven. *LA Weekly* had published a story about the massive parties, concerts, and heroin use—among other things—that went on there. It painted an image of junkies with needles in their arms laid out on the lawns along with drunken musicians, tattoo artists, and mistresses (bondage and discipline specialists). Indeed, the original manager (when I moved in) was busted for stealing and replaced by a woman who was also a lifelong addict on methadone and had a helper who was on and off heroin during her governance.

For me, moving to the Robertson Apartments was the real beginning of me using my skill set on all levels. It was within a few months of moving back there, that I began working as a psychic professionally. I consider it part of God's training program for me. It was a low place steeped in so much of everything: joy, hate, fear, degradation, creativity, love, conflict, addiction, rage, and struggle. It was rich in all the things that make life good, bad, and savory.

The Slayer's Pact: You Can Only Serve One Master

As you embark on this conscious path to self-awareness via demon slaying, it is important to understand that your sixth sense—intuition, empathy, psychic ability, instinct, or whatever you call it for yourself—is being activated. All of those descriptors that I just mentioned have slightly different definitions as they are recognized at different vibrations, but they are all related, and everyone has them. Your awareness of yourself, others, and your environment all become heightened. You begin to see things in patterns, whether it be intellectually or emotionally, and you start to understand and see things about others that they may not have directly told you. The smart watcher will hold his or her tongue.

However, it's not natural to hold this awe-inspiring and instantly acquired information quietly as you discern what it is and the wisdom it brings—especially if you're an emotional person. So, it is imperative that you don't blurt things out to others and that you don't give people information about themselves that they may not want. The other big thing here is that even though the information you receive intuitively may seem clear as a bell and in your mind may seem to clearly pertain to someone specific, you must remember that all the information that you receive is interpreted through your filters of experience and expression. *It may not mean for them, what it means to you.*

The Alpha and the Omega

Spirit before the body

Everyone lives in his or her own universe, living their personal truth. It is through this personal knowledge and experience that you will eventually align with the greater universe and the truth, which is the oneness that connects us all to the Creator.

In the beginning, there was you and where you began. That originating thought-form inspired all that you are, including the physical form you have today. This thought-form can present itself to you as many things. It can show up as a spirit guide, what others say and think about you, your past-life images (Akashic records), your dreams or desires, your lovers and friends, and your karma just to name a few. As you begin to open yourself to your inner mystery, bits and pieces will begin to fit together as the jigsaw puzzle that is you, and they will begin to take shape in your mind and heart.

Getting to this original thought-form can be your soul/sole purpose, with everything else being secondary. Seeking deeply this original thought-form, this purpose, can take a lifetime, or several. It leads you on a trail of building external things, using this deepest of essence within you, just so that you can recognize yourself from the outside. The deeper you dig, the richer the essence is, and the more it allows you to connect and understand the world you live in.

> Nothing is for free, except the freedom to command what you will pay. Never lose; only surrender.
>
> Nguvu Jabari

I am not a queen; I am a leader of the free world

Interesting things happen to people when they believe others have power over them in some way. I had lived at the Robertson Apartments almost anonymously for about six years. I didn't know a soul, as I had kept myself isolated from the other tenants, rudely turning down invitations to get acquainted. The place was deeply haunted, something I took quiet comfort in.

I was into my fourth year of working as a spiritualist when 9/11 happened and I sensed that things in my business would get slow. I heard Ben from the management company say that the manager of the building had taken ill and needed to step down. It was kismet that he was standing outside of my apartment when he said it. I took the opportunity to walk out, introduce myself, and throw out a quick pitch for becoming the new manager and in so doing became part of a new spiritual legacy for this infamous, little apartment complex that was a spiritual nexus for the neighborhood.

Every manager going back at least to 1972 had been a drug addict or alcoholic. Luckily, I was a lifetime out of that, but that's not to say I didn't enjoy happy hour on occasion. In fact, I started a Tuesday evening meeting with a few of the tenants that we called the Happy Hour Prayer Group. We talked about spiritual themes, had wine and snacks, and at the end visualized our prayers for the world and the property.

Things began to change rapidly. Day one, as the on-site manager of the Robertson Apartments, I became *The Man*. Who knew? Many of these people I hadn't yet met, and they still began by addressing me with resentment and disdain, just because I was now the manager. The neighbors with whom I shared a wall and with whom I hadn't had many interactions, were getting ready to move and threw a party that night. Almost the whole complex was invited.

I was shocked out of my sleep at about one a.m. to the partygoers chanting and pounding. It was partially the crashing of two paintings that fell from my wall that made me see what it really was on the other side of that wall: a band of merry demons with red eyes. *Oh my*, I thought, *what have I gotten myself into?*

Many of the tenants still struggled with addiction, but it was also a place where people came to find themselves, be creative, and get clean—a spiritual launch pad of sorts. I quickly learned that when people left the Robertson Apartments they always went on to better things and better lives and sometimes a better place—no matter if they had been kicked out, had left of their own accord, or God saw fit to take them.

The Slayer's Pact: **You Can Only Serve One Master**

Let me again reiterate that this place was layered with decades of spiritual energy—entities from other dimensions, grief, pain, and creativity—imprints going back to the 1920s. Apparently it had become a spiritual drop-off at which people came specifically to get something or leave something behind, physically and spiritually. The decades of lost souls, lost entities, and layers of trauma attached to the buildings and the land. Never before had anyone come to clean it up.

Over approximately the next decade that was my job.

At the time, I was going through a personal genesis of my own. I had begun my healing practice, serving clients all over the world; for the first three years, I literally worked almost 24/7. I did it with great joy but found there were a few downsides. I didn't sleep much, was constantly under spiritual attack, had an enormous amount of anxiety, and wasn't taking care of myself as well as I could. Oh, and I rarely went out into the public.

I was exhausted, in grief all of the time, and while I had quite a bit of support, I wasn't really surrounded by people who in any way had my best interests at heart. I really needed help. Every night I prayed with Jesus and St. Michael to reawaken in me the force of God. I was so weary.

The chill that night was intense, so I wrapped myself up tightly in my unicorn blanket and cried myself to sleep. Somewhere in the midst of the night I became aware of feeling warm and safe. A man had come to me—in spirit, of course—but he felt solid and real.

He was a man who lived at the beginning of time, at least a time so far and distant I couldn't really conceptualize it. Nguvu Jabari was his name. He wore a leather loincloth and had long dreadlocks grown over a lifetime, adorned with bones and beads. He had what looked to be sharp, wooden teeth, and at the time I didn't really understand the significance of the teeth. But what I did understand was that this being had fought and won many battles. Even his scars were comforting. Nguvu spoke his wisdom to me for the remainder of the night. He told me about what it was like to live the slayer's path and showed me how to feel safe in the presence of evil. He was several feet taller than me and lay behind me with his richly robust muscles conforming to my body, his arms around me so tightly that I was able to sleep peacefully for the first night in months.

> From that point on, I began to understand that Nguvu Jabari had always been present in my life, supporting me with immense bravery, cunning awareness, force, and whimsy.

The sun broke over the horizon, and for a brief moment I awoke with him still with me. As the dawn pushed her way into the day he disappeared, but the strength and peace he brought stayed. From that point on, I began to understand that Nguvu Jabari had always been present in my life, supporting me with immense bravery, cunning awareness, force, and whimsy. Every moment he had risen up to champion me came flooding back: memories from my childhood of escaping the wiles of a predator or other children's failed attempts to bully me, all the way to my life in New York City and warding off would-be attackers with the raise of my finger—all those times that I knew and understood the presence and the force of God but had yet to directly meet his emissary. Those were the things he taught me.

The invitation

Invitations to a demon come in all forms, from the direct, "Hey, come on in," to "Hey, you're angry, I'm angry, let's be angry together." It is important to understand that demons don't care. They work and live in a military structure using fear and intimidation to manipulate any situation. The strong ones rise to the top and always have minions.

Every demon has a nature, and it is the nature that is the temptation. Each demon's nature can be viewed as a variation of one or more of the biblically inspired seven deadly sins: greed, pride, gluttony, anger, lust, sloth, and envy. All of these earthly desires connect in some way to the emotions that we feel as humans, guilt being the consistent connection. The temptation itself is not really the issue. The issue is how we relate to it.

One day, my sister invited me to dinner. Although we lived in the same city, we did not see each other often. Being the baby of the family, I was always excited to be included. As I pulled up to the parking structure of her apartment building, I noticed another car directly behind me. In it was a dude with past-the-shoulder wavy and slightly wispy black hair. I think he caught my eye because when I glanced at him, I saw a skeleton—not particularly an uncommon occurrence for me so I didn't give it another thought. Her building had unique, not run-of-the-mill folk: from trannies to mistresses to corporate execs. While all extraordinary people in their own right, unusual nonetheless.

I pulled in and got out of the car. Walking towards my sister's, I noticed this man following me. I had lived in NYC so I was ultra-aware of everything going on in an environment, especially parking lots.

He must be a tenant, I thought.

I said hello and we walked to my sister's apartment together.

Hmmm, she didn't say she was inviting someone else to dinner.

His name was Bob, and as I got a closer look, the skeleton frame of his face seemed to fill in with pale ruddy skin and the darkest circles I had ever seen under any one's eyes.

My sister's apartment was one large room with the bedroom cordoned off by a low metal rail. The kitchen, dining, and living area were marked by their furniture. Bob and I sat at the dining table and were promptly served a glass of wine. My sister then stood with her back to us at the kitchen counter preparing the food for the remainder of the time until dinner was served. A dinner, by the way, I don't really remember at all.

> I then explained to Bob that it was his choice, and that no one could help him until he was ready to let go and live in another way. He would have to be ready to grieve and risk his fear of loneliness, and he understood.

Bob and I started off with the, *So what do you do?* He was in the tech industry. Evidently my reputation preceded me as my sister had told him that I was a psychic healer and that I could help him.

Okay, now it all made sense. "Help you with what?" I asked.

And then he began. "About four years ago, I wanted to know if demons really existed. So I asked if any demons really existed, then show me. Give me proof. And one night very shortly after, one came. I haven't slept soundly since."

"Wow", I responded. "Do you believe now?"

"Yes."

"Are you ready to get rid of them?"

"Yes."

"Okay. Tell him I want to talk to him. What is his name?"

Just for the record, demons are liars, tricksters, manipulators, and deceivers. That is just what they do. So when I asked for his name, he gave me something, like Beelzebub. Of course he wasn't Beelzebub so we went back and forth a few times to come up with his name and how many friends he had with him.

He had quite a few, hundreds in fact. (Demons organize in a military structure: generals, lieutenants, etc.) I asked why he was haunting Bob.

"Because he asked."

Fair enough. Now keep in mind that demons often are vulgar; they curse, call names, and accuse. This time was no different. He said a few vulgar things, called me weak, and said that he would never leave.

Oh, and my sister was still cooking, wearing an apron and everything.

I told Bob's "friend" that his time was up; he and his people had to go. I called St. Michael the archangel into our circle. He is the patron saint of warriors, and our circle was the connection of intent that Bob and I formed in order to release him of these demons.

I stood behind Bob. As he took off his hat he felt embarrassed about his thinning hair. Evidently he had lost most of it from the stress of the last four years. I placed my hands on his head and began to breathe and focus the light through my hands. Bob's face turned red and the veins in his neck were expanding and protruding. The light was overwhelming through my body.

It was awesome.

I saw hundreds of them leave. It was as if they were being beamed up to the mother ship. Bob was literally writhing back and forth, squirming uncontrollably, and trying to catch his breath.

I said his name, "Bob, breathe. Breathe. You are okay. You are safe. Breathe."

Immediately he began to calm. His breathing became deeper. The red color drained from his face and his pulse rate slowed.

And Betty Crocker over there was *still* cooking and had *no* idea!

I removed my hands from the top of his head and took my seat across from him once again. I asked him how he felt.

"Sad," he said.

I told him that was natural; no matter how bad the relationship was you always miss it when it's gone—until you grieve your loss. He really did seem much lighter, but something was still off.

"Bob, did they *all* leave?" I asked,

He laughed. "No. How did you know?"

"Who's left, Bob?"

"The General."

"Why is he still here?"

"Because I don't want him to leave," he admitted.

I then explained to Bob that it was his choice, and that no one could help him until he was ready to let go and live in another way. He would have to be ready to grieve and risk his fear of loneliness. He understood.

My sister came over to the table with full plates of her hard work. I know we ate dinner, but I don't remember anything after that.

I never saw Bob again.

The seduction

Demons first watch their unassuming prey. They make themselves known through subtle haunting—a *whoosh* here or a bump in the night there. They go where you go and watch and wait, looking for your idiosyncrasies and vulnerabilities, anything in your life that may be out of balance.

One bright Tuesday morning I went to run some errands. I stopped by the Big Lots to pick up some cat litter and other things. There was only one checkout lane open, and the lady was working diligently to help everyone quickly. She was quite impressive. I was about fifth in a line of ten.

Behind me was a young man who looked around fifteen. I noticed him because the energy around him was strong and on the creepy side. It made me stand up straight and open the eyes in the back of my head. He was a sweet-faced boy with a striped shirt and little pudgy belly. He was buying himself lunch or snacks, which consisted of some brightly colored beverages, some snack corn, and some Skittles.

As he was standing behind me, I felt him all of a sudden get agitated and frustrated at the checker's pace. He was swaying from one foot to the other as the pressure was building, and then it set its sights on me.

Under his breath the boy said to me in a deep, lurid tone, "So, do you have a pussy?"

It was loud enough for others to hear, but no one seemed to. Keep in mind that I was purchasing cat litter, but that's not what he meant. And, ya know, I was just not in the mood to deal with all that, that day.

I knew the kid was being followed by something—haunted, if you will. So I stood up straight, imagined the energy around my body expanding, and I said loud enough for everyone to hear, *"Emmm, umm!"* while shaking my head no.

Then it really started. Now he was fidgety and agitated and became loud, cursing at the checker for not going fast enough, and then again he turned his aggression towards me. Honestly, I don't remember what he said although again it was sexual in nature.

Remember the other ten people in line? Now there were twenty. Still no other lanes opened up.

I turned to the young man and his friend and practically shouted. *"I said no!* Go back to where you came from!"

Despite speaking in an extremely loud and firm voice, not one person heard me accept for the checker. She seemed to be absolutely clear about what was going on and gave me a little smile and nod as if to say, *Thank you.*

At this point the boy simmered down and became quiet. As I paid for my things, he said, "I'll see *you* outside," and smiled.

I promptly took my things and walking to the car, which was close, I called upon St. Michael to deliver this young man from his friend. Just so you know, my adrenaline was pumping and I had the pricklies up and down my spine. As I was loading up my vehicle, the young man walked out of the store and looked around with a blank face, as if wondering what he was doing. He opened up the pack of corn and walked off.

It's funny: this particular location seems to be a pit stop for the low and abiding. It always feels sad in there to me. I think it's one of the places that people must go to offload their spiritual entourage.

> Remember that it is the spirit of the sin—lust, greed, envy, etc.—that inspires someone to take action. But they take such action because they don't know any better, have similar emotions, or lack self-awareness.

Is anyone vulnerable?

A demon will only have the power they are given by their human energy hosts and can be diminished or eliminated at any time. They govern the realm of influence, which is their only power; they can never control. The young man in line was vulnerable probably for several reasons: his lack of patience and self-awareness; his aggressive tendency and sexual confusion; and a general feeling of powerlessness—the inability to make his world work the way he wanted it to.

Is everyone who has those feelings vulnerable to demonic interference? *Yes, everyone is vulnerable.* But not everyone experiences these things in this way. It truly is only a select few who are the bearers of this burden in this way. Although I suspect it is often just mistaken for bad behavior.

Remember that it is the spirit of the sin—lust, greed, envy, etc.—that inspires someone to take action, but they take such action because they don't know any better, have similar emotions, or lack self-awareness. Such people do not know themselves, their heart, their desires, or their power so they align with or choose the lower remedy.

The power

Demons offer power, which is why people accept them. I have done multiple healings with people who were abused as children, abandoned, raped, or molested and in their painful time of need asked for help or wept in quiet solitude. They became energetically susceptible to the wiles of a friendly and protective critter that promises help, strength, courage, protection, and safety. And often they provide it...until they don't any more.

Demons have a completely different presence than just your normal bad feeling or feeling of power. You can never get completely comfortable in their presence, and while their energy may add a feeling of protection or strength, they are unable to offer peace or comfort. You can perceive that their influence on someone is different than if the person were merely depressed, in pain, or angry. The demonic influence has a supernatural quality to it that usually includes a person acting outside their normal, rational frame of behavior like when a confused person all of a sudden becomes extremely clear, a kind person instantly becomes mean, or a happy person becomes instantly sad for no reason.

> So if you could know four things, know the following: You have everything that you need at any given time. You always have the power of choice. You always have angelic help. You will always have all the information that you may need exactly when you need it, if you will pay attention.

It should go without saying

I'll say this just to be clear: while demons and other critters are rampant, they in no way, shape, or form take the place of, or excuse, bad behavior or affect everyone. Not everyone will be affected by the paradigm of good and evil. What we call *evil* takes many incarnations for a soul to cultivate. It is not regular.

Human beings are not evil. They can be dense, delusional, or vacant and can be possessed by demons that are evil. The energy and force of something evil takes a lot of physical energy to host, so don't worry; very few people are at risk for this kind of possession or influence. Take Hitler: I believe this is an example of demonic possession. Hitler was not evil, he was vacant. What made him susceptible to evil were his single-minded beliefs and traumas coupled with righteousness and ignorance. Probably he suffered from all of the deadly sins.

Oftentimes suicide comes to a person who is demonically possessed. From the demon's perspective, it doesn't care or have any real concern for its impact on the physical body. It moves from one person to the next and has no regard for life. Some demons can perpetuate such a dense force of apathy that it takes outside help for a person to overcome them.

The demise

While not everyone will be attacked or possessed by a demon, almost everyone will cross the path of one in their lifetime. Today, with all the changes on the planet and the magnetic shift we all are experiencing, the natural result is to bring up the lowest within us for healing on all levels. So if you could know four things, know the following: You have everything that you need at any given time. You always have the power of choice. You always have angelic help. You will always have all the information that you may need exactly when you need it, if you will pay attention.

THE CONSEQUENCES OF ONE'S FAITH IN ANOTHER IS NEVER A DEFEAT. FAILURE ONLY EXISTS WHEN WE ABANDON THOSE WE LOVE.

STEPHEN J. MILLER, THE KEEPERS OF MANA'AN

Know Yourself, Be Protected

It all starts with you

Being self-aware is most important. The ability to discern your opinions and feelings from those around you, being clear about your own integrity, and having a moral and social compass will help anchor you in compassion and love when it comes to dealing with otherworldly critters. There is an old adage, *If you stand for nothing, you will fall for anything.* Today we have permission to assist in the healing of the planet and her inhabitants, even those without bodies. By *permission* I mean universal support.

The magnetic shifting of the planet is no longer holding certain dense or lower vibrational mental or emotional constructs. Take greed as an example. Greed is a product of lack. When folks are fearful of not having enough, they tend to save, hoard, steal, deceive, manipulate, and any other number of things. So it is important to be able to be honest with yourself as to your own tendencies. If you are a hoarder, then eventually you must purge, and any thought, feeling, belief, or entity that encourages you not to purge is working against you and must be elevated.

Demons don't necessarily elevate. They evolve, but do not elevate. Demons are energy, and energy doesn't go away; it changes form. Demons are ultimately light, and with angelic help, can be transformed into another energy with light and forgiveness. As a demon slayer your first weapon of choice is your sense of humor. It is extremely important to learn not to take yourself and others too seriously. Believe it or not, this is a skill that can be cultivated. Demons attack any vulnerability you may have, and the easiest vulnerability to attack are those beliefs and definitions that you may have about yourself, who you are, and your value.

Laughter really is the best medicine

Wellness research has proven that laughter boosts hormones like beta-endorphins, which elevate mood, and human growth hormone, which helps boost immunity. A hard-core belly laugh can also lower harmful stress hormones like cortisol, which triggers an increase in belly fat, and adrenaline, which can weaken the immune system when it stays elevated. A good laugh has even been shown to decrease bad cholesterol while increasing good cholesterol.

Laughing can also lower your blood pressure too. Energetically, the heart opens or expands when we laugh and allows for all of the other energy centers (*chakras*) to release denser energies and align with the higher frequencies that enter the body. Laughter doesn't mean that everything is okay; it just means that everything is the way it is and you are going to draw to you a way to resolve it. By the time we become adults, we have learned to censor our humor out of respect for an awful situation or for the sensibilities of others. Sometimes we see laughter as something hurtful. Don't get me wrong. There are definitely people out there who would use laughter to promote a power struggle or to imply humiliation, but then aren't they the butt of the joke? Being a little irreverent allows for us to detach from the current perspective we hold regarding our transition and its impact on us, while also allowing us to set aside any fear we may have about the current situation and transition.

IT IS ONLY THE WISEST AND THE STUPIDEST THAT DO NOT CHANGE.

CONFUCIUS

What is detachment?

Detachment is the experience of letting go of a preconceived idea and creating something to put in its place. When you experience detachment the brain is creating new neural circuitry and strengthening or weakening existing neural circuits. Our neural circuits basically tell us how we experience life based on what we have experienced before. So in order to change your mind, you must change how your brain tells you how to experience something new. Every thought we have supports the creation of something new and strengthens or weakens a preconceived idea. Every laugh stimulates and promotes this process.

The chortle

You must be completely honest with yourself about the situation in question. This includes taking into consideration other people's perspectives and comparing them to the reality at hand. The chortle laugh is centered in the head and throat and expands the throat chakra, allowing a better flow of communication.

The guffaw

Acceptance of the current reality allows you to become empowered in it and to make any necessary changes. The guffaw laugh is centered in the belly, expands the second and third chakras, and will help you release your fear of not being able to control the situation, allowing you to find an empowering position in it.

The chuckle

Forgiveness of the situation allows you to become detached from the reality and supports your awareness to create something new and better in its place. The chuckle is centered in the heart, the place in the physical body where we create hormones of peace and the energy center where we align with our higher self. The chuckle opens the heart, allowing for a stronger flow of energy to the rest of the system.

ONE MUST LEARN TO FORGIVE AND NOT TO HOLD A HOSTILE, BITTER ATTITUDE OF MIND WHICH OFFENDS THOSE ABOUT US AND PREVENTS US FROM ENJOYING OURSELVES; ONE MUST RECOGNIZE HUMAN SHORTCOMINGS AND ADJUST HIMSELF TO THEM RATHER THAN TO BE CONSTANTLY FINDING FAULT WITH THEM.

NAPOLEON BONAPARTE

The Slayer's Ritual:
Making the Most of Your Humor

Even if you are not in a place to find things funny, or even if you are surrounded by a bunch of sad sacks you do not want to offend, now is the time to take the comedy reins. Research proves the pathetic findings that children laugh three hundred to four hundred times a day versus adults who only laugh about fifteen times. Probably only a few of those are actual laughs while the rest are smirks while you're sitting in your quiet solitude thinking to yourself, *That's funny.*

We know that our responses follow our thoughts, our thoughts follow our emotions, and our emotions follow our spirit. Creating a slight shift in perspective on any one of these levels will create change in all of them.

Answer these five questions:

- What do you think about most of the time?
- Why do you think of it so often?
- What feelings are provoked when you think of it?
- Where do you feel it in your physical body?
- Would you like a change of perspective on this subject?

Now, that you have a connection to your thoughts and their impact, it's time to do something about it. For the next seven days, do your own research. Find and watch something funny five times a day, beginning first thing in the morning at breakfast time and ending just before bed. Today, with technology as it is, we have access to so much so easily. Keep a journal, and at the end of every day document how the additional humor impacted you.

The Slayer's Altar:
Understanding the Impact

The mental and emotional impact of creating an altar

Always, when creating a sacred space in your home, there is some sort of an impact. You'll get what you want, so it's important to completely understand what that means. If you're looking for peace in your life, you've got to let go of the emotions that don't allow the space for peace, which might mean feeling sadness or grief for a period of time. Or, if you're looking for a new job or to lose weight, the issue may have nothing to do with the donuts but with other, less comfortable things that you need to think about. Either way there is a trade-off: letting go of one thing in order to create space for another.

Take some time to sit and breathe deeply and contemplate what Nguvu Jabari is for you. Allow one thing you'd like to let go of to make your life better and more peaceful to come to your mind. Write your response on a piece of paper. Now clear and clean a space for your sacred altar. On the back of the paper write the affirmation below:

- I am safe, powerful, and aware. The force of the Creator is with me at all times.

What you will need:
- A white candle and a bowl of tobacco, corn, or water as an offering of gratitude.

PART 2
Breathe Deep

Demons can disappear as quickly as they came

The Slayer's Weapons:

Faith, Worship, Hyper-Vigilance,
Non-Judgment, Ruthless Compassion, Truth

The Story of Curandera Negra: Truth Creates Freedom

The thick scent of the blooming jasmine by night and the gardenia by day made it seem like a pleasant place to happen upon, but there was always something else detectible in the air, a sort of mourning. The mocking-birds continuously sang their song, except for maybe a few hours in the afternoon, really the only time to nap in peace. What were once small slave quarters far up and covered by the hills was now the home of Curandera Negra, a freed, black healer from what is now Haiti.

She was born Marie Dessalines and had all but given up her history sometime before the revolution in that country. She was smuggled into Louisiana in the dead of night and now only had her reputation to reveal her as a witch to some and as a healer to others, but absolutely powerful to all. She flat-out frightened people.

On the outskirts of New Orleans, on a plantation along the Mississippi, sat a little cottage deep in the land where the brush and trees were thick, with a little creek running right through it. The cottage had almost been forgotten. The last time it was inhabited was sometime after the slaves had been freed—freed but not necessarily free.

No one ever approached the curandera unless they needed to. She was a formidable woman standing six feet tall and boasting a rotund, buxom figure. She wore her hair as she wanted, growing free in a moder-ately short Afro. Her style was meant to blend in: flowered muslin dresses and comfortable working shoes although you could often see her on the hill at dawn and at dusk wearing her black velvet ceremonial cloak.

No one knew of her heritage, and she thought it was better that way. She had been taught two things: how to hide who you are and how to see the truth. You can never hide who you are to someone who is willing to see the truth.

People who needed her came from miles around and kept her in plenty, bringing her food and household goods. Everything else she was able to garnish from the land and environment. She made medicines from roots and herbs and detected afflictions of the spirit, but most of all it was the impact of her words. When the curandera spoke over you, things happened. That is what frightened people the most, at least the ones who could see her. She was the best kept secret in the region.

It was now the vernal equinox, and another spring was dawning, a most busy time for the curandera. Springtime always brought out the confusion in people. And summer...well, it really brought out the rage. In summertime, whatever was afflicting them seemed to float to the surface, a long, continual full moon of sorts.

The curandera would sit on the porch of her cottage in this beautifully crafted, wooden rocking chair that made even her feel petite and safe. She'd sit there for hours rocking herself into the deep, deep crevices of her spirit world that offered her access to the wisdom of the ages. The chair is where she would have many of her visions, seeing into the nature of things.

On this day, she witnessed a scene in a place she'd not been before. Only the trees seemed familiar. It was an urban city where the roads seemed to be hard, flat, and gray, covered in some places with shiny black. On each side of the road were walkways made of dull, smooth rock. Standing on one of those walkways she saw two boys and a girl. They were standing at a crossroads where there were three possible paths. In her vision, the curandera saw that the girl was wearing a very short, tight skirt; a white cotton cloth shirt; long, white and black striped socks that stayed all the way up past her knees; and a pair of work boots. The two boys, each around the age of fifteen, were wearing long, black pants that fit tight around the ankle. They all had rich olive skin and the same longish hair style. The curandera found it interesting.

> She was born in Haiti and was taught two things: how to hide who you are and how to see the truth—because you can never hide who you are to someone who is willing to see the truth.

As she traveled deeper into the nature of things, her mind's eye fell smoothly into the place just above her heart. The more deeply she breathed, the more that place in her heart began to expand. The warmth began to breed focus and clarity. Then all of that energy moved to her eyes and they became beams of light and the nature of things became obvious. It became a movie in her mind.

As she witnessed the three young'uns, she saw the direction they were headed and knew that to continue down that road in that direction would lead to darkness. For down that road were three young men all dressed in white cotton shirts and pants made of a baggy, blue fabric. She thought that was interesting too. It wasn't what they were wearing that was important, it was what she saw in their faces and attached to their bodies. They were smoking and drinking spirits, but she'd never seen what they were smoking before. It brought out something mean and cruel in these boys, something she had seen a hundred times. Its force gave her shivers. The curandera soon understood that if the boys and girl continued in that direction, the girl would be violated by all three men, and one of the boys would lose his life trying to defend her.

Curandera Negra looked for another way. If the boy who would be murdered left his friends and walked west, then he would live, but the girl would still be violated and the other boy would die. If they all walked west, then the result would be the same as that of the first path. If they all walked east, then it would be a slightly different event. The first boy would be hit by a long, blue vehicle, and within thirty days the girl would be violated by the same group of young men.

The curandera was tired. Her breathing slowed and for a moment became labored. She had spoken to God about this before. *What is the point?* Why did she have to see it all when she couldn't do anything?

God answered, "Courage."

The light from the curandera's eyes filled her whole body. She took a long, deep breath and blew the winds of courage straight into each of the young'uns' hearts, and a fourth path opened up. In that moment, it seemed time had stopped. She could still smell the subtle sweetness of the gardenias and feel the light getting low in the sky. The young'uns seemed frozen in her mind for what seemed like hours, until the girl sighed with a full exhale.

"I've got some homework to get to; you guys don't have to walk me home."

"Are you sure?" they both asked.

"Definitely."

"Hey!" one of the boys suddenly shouted. "Isn't that Jaden and Mike in the car?"

"Go catch them," she said. "I'll see ya later."

The curandera opened her eyes and exhaled, held her heart, and wept for the girl, asking again, "What is the purpose of this?"

The Creator replied, "To carry the burden of inaction is worse than any wrong action taken. This young lady cannot live with the burden of the consequences she would face from sharing her destiny with the others. You have given her the courage she needed to see that. She is who you are, Marie; you have saved your own soul."

The curandera took one final breath and as she exhaled she came back to the porch and her favorite rocking chair. With a sigh, she thought, *It's getting to be about suppertime, and that chicken's not going to catch itself.*

THE CHANGING OF BODIES INTO LIGHT, AND LIGHT INTO BODIES, IS VERY CONFORMABLE TO THE COURSE OF NATURE, WHICH SEEMS DELIGHTED WITH TRANSFORMATIONS.

ISAAC NEWTON

Demons and the Family Curse

There is a connection between people and demons. Over the course of history, human beings have evolved, as have demons, and in deep times of turbulence people have tried to protect themselves by calling on demons and other entities to do their bidding and fight their battles.

All the rumors you've heard are true: people do summon demons and send them to wreak havoc on others. People do send bad energy and intent, roots to hold you in a negative pattern. Yes, family curses exist. Curses and other mojos all have the same thing in common: they are forms of energy sent to teach a lesson, no matter who started them or why. We call this an *energetic construct* and it can be intentional or unintentional.

A family curse is an intended boundary to be realized by current and future generations. Let's say your uncle gets cursed by someone he wronged. And during the course of his life, he doesn't make any changes to himself or get the intended message. The curse will stay with his soul and be transferred down to younger generations of his family until it can be reconciled.

Do you remember in *The Color Purple*, when Celie (played by Whoopi Goldberg) points three fingers at her divisive, abusive husband and says, "Until you do right by me, everything you think about is gonna crumble"?

In fact, it does.

Now, it's easy to understand how people, when they are in a powerless position, will seek to exert their power and force in the unseen realms and sometimes call on the masters of those realms for assistance. It really makes perfect sense, over the course of history, especially in times of extreme lack and degradation. The important thing for you now to consider is that just because someone throws it at you doesn't mean you have to catch it.

In order for a curse to have any effect, *you still have to catch it.*

People who do bad things have been cultivating their inability to empathize with others and justify their desire to do harm, whether the harm is spiritual, mental, emotional, or physical. Oftentimes these people are supported by, or are vulnerable to, demonic realms when they are in this state of numbness.

Once you understand the nature of the energy that is being focused on you, or where the energy originates, then you can become clear regarding your internal dynamic that is allowing you to connect with the curse. Your problem is never the person doing the cursing; your problem is releasing the curse itself. Doing battle with the messenger only renders you more powerless than you may already feel. Your willingness to look at what the energy is and how it connects to you is the only real way out.

You are the center of power.

> Fear is ours to use and wield at our own discretion; it does not control us; we control it. It is important to remember who's in charge: you are...always.

The Slayer's Path: Hypervigilance is the New Black

A person who has been abused in any way opens up a path of telepathy with his or her abuser. The person learns to feel and witness the signs they hope will keep them safe and avert the expected attack. They become aware of small facial expressions, called micro expressions, they've witnessed when their abuser begins to escalate into a path of aggression.

It is the same way for the spiritual realm. You can gain a subtle awareness when there is something energetically dense, mean, or evil present. Sometimes people experience smells or temperature changes or a sense of dread and anxiety in their gut when a critter is present, and they will relate all of these things to their abuser because abusive people are often influenced by, or vulnerable to, demons and other critters.

There are three themes going on in my head right now: hypervigilance, the use of language to stir up drama (judgment) and support that hypervigilance, and living in a delusion and the power and density of hatred.

The Slayer's Path:
Hypervigilance is the New Black

I have had many people ask me how to deal with the constant barrage of terrorism and the fear it seeks to promote. The answer is that fear is a tool that makes us more consistently aware of ourselves, others, and our surroundings in order to survive. It is ours to use and wield at our discretion. It does not control us; we control it. It is important to remember who's in charge: you are—always.

In the beginning, fear was born to be our personal bodyguard, to save us from occurrences of destruction on any level. Today it has evolved to become our personal alarm system alerting us of any possibility of change. How you feel the fear gives you an indication on what level of energy—physical, etheric, emotional, mental, or spiritual—you are being threatened; that is, there is an agent of destruction beginning to infiltrate you on some level that is recognized by the fear. Being an agent of destruction does not mean that something is bad or that it can, or will, destroy you; it means that it is opposing your current philosophy and ideals, or it will create some possibly irrevocable change. We feel extreme fear in times of irrevocable change, no matter if it is for the better or for the worse.

> It is important to understand that a person under the influence of otherworldly forces needs your support and strength to overcome them, not your beatdown.

The Slayer's Pact: Never Go Looking for a Fight

A slayer never goes looking for a fight, because she knows intrinsically that life can be an immense struggle for some. Your ability to show compassion for others being exactly where they're at is a skill that takes time and practice to develop. It is important to understand that a person under the influence of otherworldly forces needs your support and strength to overcome them, not your beatdown, which will only diminish their ability to fight the spiritual battle they are in.

I understand that it is easy to feel caught off guard or frightened when someone you know or cross paths with is afflicted, but it is in no way an excuse for an angry or frightened response. It is imperative to learn to distinguish between the critter and the human soul under attack.

The Slayer's Pact: **Never Go Looking for a Fight**

Many years ago, because I was extremely empathic and open to emotional connection with everything, I was an easy energetic target, be it from demons or humans. I was in a relationship with a man who I believe was under attack from his previous relationship. He, I, and his son had deep karmic ties. I believe the very reason for our relationship was so that I could meet his son, just once.

The last few months of the relationship were difficult as I was certain attacks had begun. We'd be getting along fabulously in our conversations over the phone, but when I would see him in person, I would immediately feel upset and tearful, and he'd be filled with anger and disdain. The minute our eyes met the conflict began. I can still remember the look on his face and in his eyes: one of total disdain for which there was no logical reason.

> To carry the burden of inaction is worse than any wrong action taken.
>
> Marie Dessalines

Again, my vulnerability was my capacity for emotion. I would immediately feel the shift from joy to immense grief and fear. My boyfriend didn't really understand the dramatic change of my demeanor, nor was he aware of the energy coming from him. I want to reiterate here that what he exuded and how I felt was not rational or connected to any real-world issue that we had, but our interaction generated strong and overwhelming power. Some other person's intention had added an additional, negative force to our relationship and it wasn't anyone I knew.

During that time I had a friend I shared these things with; she was the only one I knew who understood them. Unable to recover from the emotional distress I was in, I called her. A man close to her answered the phone. I was at an incredibly low point of despair and just couldn't get out of it. When he heard my voice asking to speak with her he began to curse violently at me, yelling and screaming to leave him and his family alone. His yelling continued for what felt like several minutes. I am not certain how that call ended.

All I remember is hanging up the phone and being in an even more diminished position than where I started. In my low way, it took me several days to recover from his reaction to me, to get back to dealing with the real issue at hand. It is not uncommon for a person who is afflicted in some way to be influenced easily by the energy that is their own trigger. In this case, mine was grief and his was anger. That was the most valuable information cultivated from this experience. Having self-awareness and learning to do no more harm is the greatest tool of a slayer.

It is possible for the afflicted or the slayer to set boundaries with the demonic spirit and strengthen the soul under attack. In order to do that, one must demystify the archaic understanding of certain spiritual concepts.

> We suffer the most about the things that we have the least awareness of.

Sorcery

The definition of *sorcery* is the action of commanding the power of evil spirits for various uses, such as divining the future. This definition is from the 1400s; today, sorcery has a completely different meaning.

It is true that demons and otherworldly critters often have vision, but their vision is no different than our ability to be clair-audient, clairvoyant, or clair-sentient. This is the reason that the psychic realms get such a bad rap and why so many experience those dimensions of energy as dangerous: demons and other critters simply have abilities that many of us haven't developed.

There is a hilarious scene in the movie, *The Devil's Advocate* where the Devil confronts a young thug on a subway train who is about to mug someone. The Devil speaks to him in Spanish and tells him his wife is having sex with his neighbor. It stops the guy cold in his tracks, as he recognizes the truth in it. The mugger, looking frantic, immediately heads out of the train.

It is a common misunderstanding that once you open to the spiritual realms, you can irrevocably get stuck in one of them. The truth is that ultimately, on a spiritual level, you choose where you go and what you do—like the thug on the subway—and it is rare that a person chooses that stuck path for a lifetime. Although we see it in our sanitaria and mental facilities, it is not common in comparison to how many people open up consciously and unconsciously to these realms every day and remain safe and intact. Also, consider what may be gained from such a spiritual journey.

The idea of sorcery originates from the energetic emotional center of the body, which contains the second chakra and governs the genitals, which is the seat of all delusions, desires, and strong creative forces. The frequency of this bodily region forces inspiration and creativity from the higher self into physical manifestation through the emotions.

As a part of the creative process, the emotions help us imagine consequences through feeling. An architect imagines a building and as a part of the creative process discerns what it should look like in relation to where it's going and what it will be used for. Whether or not the architect is consciously aware of it, this imagination and feeling are a natural part of the process.

The second chakra is also the seat of addiction. Addictive behavior happens when there is a continual loop of the same idea being generated over and over again with the illusion that it is changing. When your emotions alone generate an idea it stays stagnant and in the same condition or state in which it was created. Ultimately, it is necessary that all emotions be illuminated by the frequency of higher chakras: power and instinct (third chakra), the heart (fourth chakra), the voice (fifth chakra), the intuitive (sixth chakra), or the visionary center (seventh chakra). This process of the creative transformation is what allows the idea to become manifest in its highest and best form. If any of the steps are passed over, then the idea may become manifest with consequences that need to be overcome by taking you through a conscious process of traversing the centers of awareness that were missed. You will always begin this process of traversing missed steps at your lowest common denominator.

> If you are asking for a new car or the love of your life, but you're used to owning a hoopty or being with a lover that cheats and steals, then it is possible that there is a mental, emotional, or spiritual gap between what you want and what you are able to handle.

The Principal of the Lowest Common Denominator

Many ancient religions and rituals were created to instill in their followers the discipline and self-knowledge necessary for spiritual growth. For example, the awareness it takes to manage $100 is not the same awareness it takes to manage $10,000 or $100,000. If there is a deficit in managing $100, then that deficit will be amplified in managing $10,000 or $100,000.

It is the same for you spiritually. If you are asking for a new car or the love of your life, but you're used to owning a hoopty or being with a lover that cheats and steals, then it is possible that there is a mental, emotional, or spiritual gap between what you want and what you are able to handle. In that gap or space is the information needed to obtain your desire. This is called the principle of the lowest common denominator.

In times of stress you will always resort back to the lowest common denominator of your thinking and feeling patterns. To upgrade, the lowest common denominator is where you begin. It is not important whether you know what the lowest common denominators are for yourself at this point, but it is incredibly important that you understand we begin to consciously acknowledge this through our judgment. The purpose of judgment is to help us understand our preconceptions of ourselves. Judging others can help us be clear on our vulnerabilities.

Judgement equals awareness

When we judge others or situations, it means that we bring our awareness to those people or situations. Most often the things that we notice and that are prevalent are the mirror image of the same undiscovered dynamic in our own life. That doesn't mean that the situation or circumstances are the same, but that the same underlying mode of operation is at work. We are critical in our judgment when our spirit and our unconscious self would like our heart and our conscious mind to become aware of something. We suffer the most about the things that we have the least awareness of.

> It has never been my experience that anyone is ever superior or inferior: there is only understanding and ownership. When you understand and take ownership of the God in you, it is inevitable to recognize it in others.

My First Job As a Psychic

The information in this book isn't really new. It is wisdom born of my familiar experiences, ones that have played out time and again before me. I just happen to be one person in a long line who've had these experiences over the centuries.

When I first began in this business, I got a job at the fairly local New Age bookstore. I had the pleasure of working every day with several other psychic people, mostly women, from all different generations. There was a woman named Rosanna, who was from Eastern Europe and used a crystal ball, so she was pretty popular.

Alondraa was the most popular psychic at the shop. She was about 5'2", weighed about a hundred pounds, and had hair blacker than night that she styled in a moderate Elvira-esque teased-back 'do. Alondraa was definitely not the Earth Mother type. She was in her sixties and had been there the longest. She came to be psychic after being struck by lightning around the tender age of five.

When business was slow we would sit in the back of the shop, chairs positioned in a circle, and laugh and talk and share information. Well, most of us would. I remember once asking Alondraa if she wanted to trade readings, and she was not interested *at all*. Energetically, there was this wall of, *You cannot have my secrets!* This was one of my first experiences dealing with other professional psychics, but the idea that one psychic could have a technique that was secret from everyone—or the idea that secrets mattered—I found fascinating.

It was a crisp January afternoon, bright and sunny with a chill in the air, an average California winter. Suga and I were the first in the circle. Suga wasn't her real name, of course. She was a beautiful Cuban native who'd been born into a family with an abusive father. Her extended family practiced Santeria complete with closet altars. By the time she and her siblings escaped to America, she had no interest in participating in any of it.

She was in her early twenties, almost a decade younger than me. That was the average age difference between all of us, about seven to ten years apart. Daisy was next in the room; it must have been a slow day if Daisy didn't have a client. She was a stunning blonde, about 5'9", who always came to work with her hair curled and wearing full makeup. She always smelled of strong pheromones, sometimes a pleasant fragrance and sometimes like she hadn't showered in days. In retrospect, I now think it may have been the grief on her that my bionic nose was picking up on. When I got to know her story, who could blame her? The fact that she got up every morning and handled her business was impressive.

Madeleine was the sensitive in the group. Everything was always too much for her most of the time. Her famous tag line was asking, "Could you pull your energy back? It's really too much." The one time Madeleine was able to brave coming with us to the bar we'd occasionally go to after work, she asked the guy next to her if he could pull his energy back. For obvious reasons she took a substantial amount of ribbing from all of us.

Then in walked Breana, a gentle, sweet spirit lovely as the breeze and full of daddy issues that she so gracefully covered up. Breana wasn't the name that she was called in high school, but it definitely represented who she was choosing to be now. Even though she laughed, I think she always felt a great compassion for whomever the joke targeted.

Next was Pauline, an amazingly compassionate channel, an itty-bitty thing; she reminded me of a hobbit. She was the angel lady. In every group of psychics there is at least one. Pauline wasn't supposed to live past the age of seven, so to have arrived in her mid-forties after at least twelve open heart surgeries and three pacemakers, she obviously had friends in very high places.

Finally, in walked Alondraa, the unmotherly matriarch of the group. Alondraa rarely had time to sit and chat with the rest of us, but this day was especially slow so we were all sitting in the circle telling our *becoming psychic* stories. For me, the thing with Alondraa was her uniqueness, or so she thought. Don't get me wrong: being struck by lightning as a young child and then becoming psychic because of it is spectacularly unique. But her attitude intimated she was better or more important or somehow separate from the rest of us.

So on that day Alondraa was telling her story, her slightly raspy voice surprisingly high for the amount of cigarettes she smoked. I'd worked at the shop for a few weeks, and it seemed customary to trade readings with all of the other ladies as a way of getting to know each other, but Alondraa wouldn't trade with me. She did, though, accept a reading from me, as if to determine whether I was competition or not. She put me off for weeks, so at this point I had not had the Alondraa experience.

At the end of her story, I said, "Hmm…so that's the crashing and banging I hear from your room at the beginning of your readings?" and then I acted as if I was being struck by lightning, with my body convulsing me into a trance and then sitting straight up in the chair as if someone else had arrived in my body to do the reading.

Alondraa's mouth dropped as the rest of us howled in uncontrollable laughter on so many levels. No one ever really addressed her directly in an unserious way. She was the undeserving matriarch, assuming the title solely by age. She was slightly bitter and selfish and it appeared that no one ever really talked to her, only behind her back. Once the shock subsided, a smile broke over her face and she began to laugh with us. It seemed for the first time she was a part of the group.

> Sometimes our goal isn't what we or others think we want for someone, because healing comes in many forms; sometimes it is not about saving a life, but saving a soul through love.

See Things As They Really Are

As for me, I became known as the demon slayer. I worked at that shop for exactly one year, and I saw myself through every single one of those women in ways I'd not yet been able to capture. Life is very different with a witness, and each one of them allowed me to see myself from a different vantage point. I learned that all of the things I made fun of, and all of the things my judgment brought my awareness to, were certainly the way others may have perceived me. At different intervals, I had experienced or was experiencing the attitudes or conditions I saw before me. I learned from Alondraa that my experiences weren't so traumatically unique; from Suga, that my relationship with Christianity was the impetus for my self-excavation; from Daisy, what it looked and felt like to others to witness my perpetual grief. From Madeleine, I witnessed the degree of sensitivity that I carried, and Breana allowed me to see the deep, reverberating impact of having lost my father so early in life.

It was an amazingly intense learning experience.

I had clients ranging from church deacons to dock workers. There was the heroin addict from the one-hour motel next door. One night a grandmother brought her sixteen-year-old grandson; I'm not sure where his mother was, but his father was incarcerated. She was hoping that somehow working with me would keep him out of a gang and off the streets. Surprisingly, he was incredibly open to our conversation. He was already in the gang and spent most of his nights hanging out. While he was open to our conversation and listened to everything I had to say, there was this force field around him—constructed out of his beliefs and possibilities—that I couldn't penetrate. *Live by the sword, die by the sword* was where he was at, and it was clear to me that is where he would stay for the duration.

That night after working with him, I cried for him during the entire thirty-minute ride home. It wasn't sadness per se, but God's way of explaining that through me, the young man got to experience love and non-judgment, emotions that characterized our exchange. Healing comes in many forms; sometimes our goal isn't about saving a life, but saving a soul through love. I think of him now and again and always hope I was wrong about his destiny. But I suspect I wasn't. It wasn't my job to change him; it was my job to accept him as he was, love him, and reiterate to him his value. I did that.

Taking Ownership

So this is how I contemplate ownership. We truly are all connected and God expresses his love and power through each and every one of us. It is our job to be accountable for that expression of love and the degree and vibration by which we express it. For every higher, there is a lower; for every negative, there is a positive. Duality is one of the ways that we explore and understand God's universe.

While we are under the influence of duality, there are specific rules that we must follow in order to have balance. The consequence for not following the rules is imbalance. Imbalance is never permanent, ever. Part of balance is seeing the big picture, expanding your philosophy and beliefs to include possibilities of limitlessness and eternity, but not every person will see the big picture at the same time. People will see it in their own time, and inevitably all will see it. This is where the idea of having multiple lives comes in. It allows us to conceptualize and accept ourselves as powerful, multidimensional beings who have had multiple experiences that give us wisdom along our path of enlightenment and evolution.

The greatest tragedy is for one to have wisdom but no voice. Our multidimensionality leads us to take joy in all things and in all ways, lifting us out of duality and into self-realization.

> For every higher, there is a lower; for every negative, there is a positive. Duality is one of the ways that we explore and understand God's Universe.

The Rules of Judgment

Rule #1

People read our energy before they physically see us. It's true that long before a person is actually in the range of physical sight, that you have already energetically and intuitively summed them up and have a feeling or instinct about them. What is important to know is that your instinct will bring up your personal information first before it relays information specifically related to the person that is in your view. That means that your issues will come to the surface first.

Rule #2

We judge other people in order to better understand our own needs, likes, or dislikes. Judging others offers us an opportunity to be objective and witness what we like and dislike in the world. If I see a girl wearing a dress that I don't think is attractive, it is because my first acknowledgement of it is to see myself in it or to bring my style and likes to the fore.

Rule #3

The things that we notice in others are the things that we have concern about within ourselves. When things get our attention in a strong, judgmental way, we are bringing to the light or to our conscious mind what we fear. When you know that's what you're doing, it makes it easier to navigate relationships. Of course, when you still believe that your judgment of others is solely about them, you endure a rocky and confusing road, for sure.

Rule #4

Judgment can be a form of protection. I am a firm believer that the original purpose of judgment was to offer critical instinctual information to keep you safe and healthy. However, because many of the recent generations were born equipped to process decades of emotion our predecessors were not able to process, judgment becomes a significant dynamic that we use to help us discern the nature of the emotions, beliefs, ideals, and philosophies that we need to let go of or expand on in order to feel, experience, and understand what our ancestors were unable to.

The Slayer's Motto: It Is Neither Fortune nor Misfortune

The most important rule of duality is learning to address everything in detachment—even demons. Detachment doesn't mean that you don't care or aren't powerful. It means that there is a deeper understanding of everything. Opening up to a new level of understanding leads you to another, which leads you to another, until inevitably you reach the truth.

There is a Chinese proverb that tells the story of a farmer who tended his land with his son until the son breaks a leg and can no longer help.

After the accident the farmer exclaimed, "It is neither fortune nor misfortune."

The next day, all the young men of the village are called to fight a war, except his son because he has a broken leg, and again the farmer exclaimed, "It is neither fortune nor misfortune."

The Slayer's Motto:
It Is Neither Fortune nor Misfortune

The mantra, *It is neither fortune, nor misfortune,* is endowed with the understanding that everything is valuable exactly as it occurs even when we are not yet standing at the vantage point that allows us to see it.

I meet quite a few people talking about getting to the end of their karmic cycle, saying things like, *I am an old soul, this is going to be my last life here,* or *I am a young soul, I don't know very much.* Being at the end of your karmic cycle doesn't dictate whether or not you remain in human form, it determines what you do out of obligation to yourself. It is my experience that old souls truly have a good time here and usually don't want to leave, reveling in the occasional weariness. And there are no *new* souls, just upgraded bodies and souls needing to learn accountability for something, possibly needing to have a limited sphere of information in order to keep their focus.

It has never been my experience that anyone is ever superior or inferior: there is only understanding and ownership. When you understand and take ownership of the God in you, it is inevitable to recognize it in others.

What Is the Devil: Illusion, Delusion, or Reality?

Now that you have a little understanding on what exactly a demon is, it's time to address the Devil. Satan is a dark angel and exists in only a few of the world religions, and he's not too important for our purposes here, either. By understanding and mastering these larger concepts about the Devil you will be able to handle Satan should he come your way.

For me, *the Devil* is not Satan. The concept of the Devil is a more comprehensive concept addressed by every philosophy, culture, and religion. Simply put, the Devil is illusion. It is all that is contained in the gap between our desire and the formation of reality, the manifestation of the physical world. As I sit here today, writing these pages, it all occurs to me as quite funny, even light and airy, as if a great wind has come and blown away all of the fear, suffering, misery, and despair that always accompanies the concept of the Devil: the great accuser—slanderer.

The entirety of this life for me has been, on most levels, always focused on the work of the spirit. I have always had the awareness of the workings of the spirit even as my human self was living life. The illusion of this separation was most potent in my early childhood as my days were filled with the activities of a child, but accompanied by the subtle manifestations of the harshness of humanity. I carried the awareness of knowledge that had not yet been gained in my living experiences.

> The concept of the Devil is a more comprehensive concept addressed by every philosophy, culture, and religion. Simply put, the Devil is illusion.

My nights were filled with active dreaming, the receiving of messages and visits from other dimensions, all before the age of six. While I definitely had excruciating fear during the occasional demonic visitations in the middle of the night, my spirit was already equipped with the *spiritual technology of prayer.*

Interestingly enough, my family was not religious at all, so prayer was one of those things that my spirit just already had. I was baptized Methodist, because that's what Mom was. Dad was atheist, as well as my sisters at the time. Mom, however, didn't go to church too often, just mainly on holidays. I would tag along to church with any of my friends who were going on any given Sunday, with two dimes in hand that Dad had given me for the offering plate.

I cannot begin to express how much love I have for churches. No doubt it is the countless hours I have spent in this life and past lives in them. It is not the Church that I love, but the buildings themselves, the broken hearts they have housed, and the revelations they have witnessed. It is the sum of the life, joy, and courage they have held within their walls— the gentle sounds of the monks' a cappella, the soothing smell of the burning pinon, frankincense, myrrh, or *nag champa* that opens the mind for renovation—that always fills me with inspiration.

For me God is everywhere I am and needs no special house; it is all the home of the Creator. That said, places that are built with the intent of self-revelation are special and sacred. Their walls are primed with God's love and hard work. Truly he expects nothing of us but for us to acknowledge our beauty and divinity. The church is where we struggle to do that, to resist the temptations of the human disbelief in our own divinity, and then inevitably to respond to the overwhelming responsibility of creating our own lives.

If you ask me, churches don't lose their power even when the Church is gone. The layers upon layers of human celebration and suffering are packed into every molecule of wood, cement, and drywall. The consistent calling upon the angels and the petitions of our highest hearts, fill each bit of space with worthy justification of standing. Even when we repurpose a church with another business, I believe its function stays the same: to generate comfort and self-revelation.

Can demons visit a church, you ask? Of course they can. Some were even born there, but make no mistake about it, God always wins. The highest intent will always prevail. There is always a powerful force, strength, and support for you in a church, whether or not you are a member or even if the Church has moved out.

I loved going to different denominational churches because it really mixed up the monotony of the different rituals. It promoted my love of ritual that is intrinsic to my spirit. The other thing that church taught me is the purpose of faith, that religion is a path to the understanding of the Creator and a path to the understanding of our human connection and relationship with the Creator. Religion is not the relationship itself. A relationship with the Creator is yours, and yours alone; it can't be shared with others in a religion.

As a child of about six or seven years old, the Lord's Prayer was an effective tool to repel the midnight demonic visitations that I was having. But, becoming a born-again Christian, and praying extra-hard proved no match for the cancer that was slowly stealing my father's vitality. When he died, I was mad at God. Why had my prayers not been heard? I was eleven at the time. I understood then what my spirit had always known, that just because God exists doesn't mean bad things won't happen and that the practice of religion can only promote and cultivate your relationship and understanding of the world and its Creator.

It is through that understanding that our mind, body, and spirit become liberated from all that binds us to our fear. In the beginning, then, fear becomes the central focus of our relationship to the Creator. Cultivating a relationship with God is then releasing ourselves from the illusion of powerlessness as human beings and recognizing our expanding awareness of the limitlessness of the image in which we were created.

Essentially, we are what God is to the extent of our ability to embrace and wield such power. Everything in between God and our ability to embrace and wield that power is the Devil, *the illusion of separation from God.*

Spiritual Supply and Demand: Do Your Beliefs and Knowledge Enable Your Goals?

Okay, I should flat out say right here you don't have to believe in God to deal with the Devil. No matter what you believe in, your spirit is leading you on a path to the reconciliation of the illusion of our human separation from the Creator of all that is. At some point it will be important for you, in this life or another, to delineate and define the connection between science and spirit and to begin to name those things that have always been in your subtle awareness. Chances are that if you are reading this, you're there now. So from here on out, I will define God and the Creator as what we connect to with our divine self, or higher self. The universe is where we live, not who we are.

Our spirit is connected to our higher self through our heart, and our higher self connects to the Creator. The slower (comparatively speaking) vibrational elements of ourselves are our thoughts, emotions, and etheric body. Those are the elements of our human experience that are susceptible to the Devil and the many forms of expression that the Devil personifies. There are times in life that you may have to reevaluate what you know and the beliefs and ideals that you hold in order to complete your goals or make your dreams come true.

It is true that being a demon slayer warrants a warrior's posture and ideals, but before we get to that, I'd like to break down for you the different kinds of spiritual entities and constructs that exist, so that you can be a little clearer on what it takes to do battle or not do battle, with each.

The Devil

I absolutely do believe the Devil exists. There are demonic dimensions that exist to which many humans have access. Now, not all people will address those dimensions, but they do in fact exist. Again, it is a matter of perception and spiritual development. All religions have a relationship with something that they consider demonic. In some religions there are even demons that serve a very important and good function, therefore rendering them at a certain point positive and purposeful.

The information that you have brought into this life will give you an indication of your own personal relationship to this concept. The Devil, however, will always be the driving force. It doesn't matter if you believe in, know of, heard of, are in fear of, or are at peace with the Devil—the Devil will always be in energy form. The Devil does not live in the physical reality, no matter how you conceptualize it; it lives in the nonphysical dimensions and only has access to our world through us.

So if it is here with you, somehow, somewhere, on some level, it is yours. The Devil deserves respect. Trying to trivialize what you don't yet know about the Devil does not protect you in any way from the Devil. All it does is leave you further away from the understanding that you need to have of it, the understanding that will eliminate your fear and free you from the Devil. Some people think that if you give respect or direct acknowledgment in any way to the Devil, then that makes you more vulnerable to the wiles of the Devil. That is not true at all.

> The Devil deserves respect. Trying to trivialize what you don't yet know about the Devil does not protect you in any way from the Devil.

The better you know and accept yourself, the more understanding you have of other spiritual dimensions and the less access the Devil has to you. I know there are many rumors out there about demons and how you can catch them, as if they were an illness. I've heard people say that you shouldn't look someone straight in the eye because it makes you vulnerable to them or to demonic possession, or that demons are passed from person to person by touch, such that if you are around someone who is afflicted you are vulnerable too. All of these theories stem from a lack of understanding about how energy works. The truth is, you can only be afflicted by demons if you are unaware of yourself or resonate with their nature in some way. We call it *agreement* and *permission*.

One evening Janna and her boyfriend Paul were at a mixer at the local drug and alcohol rehab center. It was an open event where community members could come and meet the staff and get a better understanding of the work they did. Janna worked there as a counselor and had a friendly relationship with one of the male counselors she worked with. He actually had a crush on her. This was his first time meeting Janna's boyfriend, and he showed obvious signs of disappointment, but he kept up a pleasant face as the three of them were talking.

It seemed like an amiable conversation until the male counselor spoke out, under his breath, "Yes, you guys are happy now until you overdose and die." A look of horror overtook his face as the words were leaving his lips.

Janna heard him and looked at the other counselor perplexed. Paul didn't hear him and a few moments later excused himself to get another glass of punch.

Janna immediately said, "Hey, what was that you said?"

The counselor replied, "Something really awful, I don't know where it came from. Seriously, I don't know why I said that."

They both laughed at the shock of it and then moved on to the rest of the evening as if nothing had happened.

It is common for folks who have used drugs to have a demonic posse for quite some time during recovery. In fact, that's what recovery is: the process of clearing your soul of self-destructive behavior and the entities that you often attract while using drugs and destroying yourself and others. In this situation, the counselor's disappointment in the presence of the object of his affection, as well as his lack of awareness, made him vulnerable to the strength and intensity of the demonic energy that was with Janna's boyfriend. The demon spoke through the counselor to his intended victim, Janna's boyfriend. He in fact struggled daily with his sobriety and self-destructive behavior.

Luckily, the counselor had some mastery of his own emotion and was able to keep the intrusion at bay by speaking softly, knowing on some level that the words he was speaking weren't his. In this situation, all three of them were energetically connected, the counselor to Janna, and Janna to her boyfriend. All three of them had different emotional connections and different levels of awareness. That is the dynamic that created this situation. That's why I cannot stress enough how important it is to know yourself and your limits.

Where does the devil live?

The Devil lives everywhere. How people relate to illusion is directly related to their perspective and experiences. Illusion is the same thing as creativity and imagination, depending on where you are focused. For example, if you are an emotional person, then the Devil will seek to connect to your emotions, and you will experience the broadband of illusion in the way you feel about things.

In the next chapter we will address the five basic levels of energy and discern the lenses through which they allow you to perceive the world. The perspective that you have and the type of transition you are in (as we are all in some sort of transition all of the time) will give you an indication of where the Devil lives for you. As you recognize the filters through which you witness your life, you are then able to recognize the inherent spiritual rules that govern that particular perspective. This little morsel is the key to why we sometimes have such a difficult time understanding one another, especially on a global stage. The rules for an emotional perspective are different than the rules for a spiritual one.

> You don't have to believe in God in order to deal with the Devil. No matter what you believe in, your spirit is leading you on a path to the reconciliation of the illusion of our human separation from the Creator of all that is.

We will all move through all levels of perception on our journey of spiritual development. How we move, when we move, or where we move, is what is illusive. The idea that someone is an old soul infers they have come into the world with certain, expanded spiritual perceptions on life. Make no mistake about it: there are no young souls, just the perception of innocence or immaturity. Everyone has dimensions in themselves to expand, in order to create balance and master acceptance. The ascended masters like Jesus and Buddha just did it with an audience.

This is where the concept of karma or past lives comes in handy. Every spirit comes in to this incarnation with downloads of information or memory. These pockets of energy contain all that you need to know to begin your path of spiritual development in this life. Even believing that you do not have a spiritual path is a path.

Karma, a Sanskrit word, is a Hindu concept referring to the idea that for every action there is an equal and opposing reaction. It includes—but is not limited to—the spiritual concept of duality: good and evil, light and dark, yang and yin. Karma is not simply the idea that if you do something bad, something bad will happen to you. It means if you kill someone, with that comes the complete and total understanding of its impact. This understanding does not come in what we consider to be linear time and space; it is its own dimension of time and space that we humans may relate to as a past life.

Let's say you were Attila the Hun in a past life, and you killed a hundred thousand people for what you thought was a righteous cause. Now, we can assume that Attila did not experience the remorse of killing as he was killing, that he was free from that remorse as he killed. The equal and opposing force that comes with killing a hundred thousand is the remorse for that action, a remorse that includes the energy of the event and the dimension where it took place. Can you imagine the demon of one hundred thousand cries that is attached to the spirit of Attila?

So being Attila, you have not experienced this remorse for killing one hundred thousand since the time of your death in 453 CE; you brought this download or memory into this lifetime and must now, through your experiences today, process the illusion of enormous remorse and all that comes with it. Of course, you probably are not a warlord in this lifetime, but your spirit will attract to your life today what you need in order to process the grief of that remorse and to gain spiritual understanding, insight, and forgiveness. Or, maybe you will be holed up in a sanitarium somewhere living that grief day in and day out. Can you imagine what your life might look like?

> The better you know and accept yourself, the more understanding you have of other spiritual dimensions and the less access the Devil has to you.

Critter Fest 101: Types of Energetic Afflictions

Emotional trauma

Experiencing an emotional trauma of any sort that remains unprocessed can lead to the transfer of that trauma along with the soul into other lifetimes, or to other people who resonate with it and are more equipped to process the energy through grief.

Mental illness

Many mental illnesses are indeed the result of a diseased spirit or are hauntings. A critter can transfer along with the soul through as many life experiences as it takes to be recognized and reconciled. This transference can sometimes be recognized as an actual chronic haunting such as schizophrenia or chemical imbalance like bipolar disorder that renders a person unable to fully take responsibility for his thoughts, feelings, and actions.

When this is the case, oftentimes, medication is necessary for the person afflicted, in order to avoid hurting themselves or others. It is my experience that many who are diagnosed with a mental illness are spiritually afflicted in some way. Through spiritual healing, emotional processing, grieving, and behavioral retraining, they can foster a complete recovery. Some, however, will live an entire life cycle in the bondage of a brain pattern that renders them unable to sustain themselves in some way. It is always the purpose of the spirit to regulate, heal, and bring itself back into balance, no matter how long that takes.

Depression

In general, depression is the spirit's way of creating a stasis of the senses, so that the self can process information about the spirit. It is the spiritual way to self-reflect and become aware of your personal patterns.

Post-traumatic stress disorder (PTSD)

PTSD is the soul's way of holding the information of a trauma until the person who experienced it is in a safe environment to process the information and respond to it, especially mentally and emotionally. The response can come weeks, months, years, and even lifetimes later. For some, once the trauma is reawakened, it will play over and over in an endless loop, seeking a new resolution or forgiveness. The information of the trauma will include every bit of the experience that occurred, including what happened leading up to the event, the event itself, and then everything that happened after. The traumatic stress response is the way that the conscious mind recovers and processes all of the information in all energy bodies (physical, etheric, emotional, mental, and spiritual).

Physical trauma and congenital defects

Physical traumas such as accidental death, death from unexpected illnesses, or tragic endings such as homicide or drug overdose can present in another lifetime as congenital defects, birth marks, physical trauma, and accidents early in life as a way for the soul to process emotion and gain spiritual understanding from the previous trauma. I worked with a guy once who had a scar on his leg from childhood. He was in his forties and it still, on occasion, bothered him to that day. In our session, a past life came up for him where he was a member of the Plains Tribe, wounded in battle with an arrow in the exact spot where he carried the scar. After removing the spiritual imprint of the arrow, battle, and wound, he was able to find forgiveness and understanding of the events of that lifetime; he never had pain in that leg again.

Ghosts

Ghosts are energetic imprints of people who have once lived in physical bodies. After dying, their energy is so strong that their imprint or energy memory is kept alive and acknowledged by living people. Oftentimes when we see ghosts, we tap into the dimension within their life and witness their normal life activities.

In Pasadena, California, there is a lot of spiritual history. I was called to do a house healing on a lovely 1920s home that was being renovated. The contractor was having problems on a lot of different levels on the site and knew that part of the issue was spiritual. One of the interesting things I found was the ghost of the original owner's wife. She had a little sewing room at the top of the landing of the second floor, a room in which she clearly had spent a great deal of her days.

The contractor had decided to make a closet, put a wall where the original door was, and move the door to the other side. As I approached this area she was angry and cursing at the change (as it was an interruption to the energetic pattern), doing just what she would have done had she been living. Years of repetitive behavior had left an imprint of that behavior made from her essence. The ghost was not her soul, but just an imprint of her energy body that was left behind and never cleared. There were many other spiritual elements that held that energy in place.

Earthbound spirits (discarnate)

Now, a discarnate is an actual spirit that has been disembodied and is unable to ascend back to the oversoul. Sometimes a person who dies in a traumatic way, through homicide, suicide, an accident, or drug overdose, can be disembodied so abruptly that his spirit maintains a great attachment to his current reality and therefore is unable to transition. Oftentimes these spirits must continue their work without a body, by enlisting the help of those in physical bodies to help them gain understanding.

Not every person in these positions will be unable to ascend, as sometimes it is a quick transition out of the physical reality that is a part of their destiny. Situations like suicide and drug overdose, however, usually lead the person into such a depressed state of consciousness that the disembodied spirit must first deal with all the unresolved elements before it is able to rejoin the oversoul fully. When a soul is unable to ascend, the discarnate can attach itself to another person in the physical world who aligns with the same energies and has some of the same issues. The discarnate might follow that person to the person's next physical incarnation, so that it can finish the work and understanding of the previous lifetime.

> Situations like suicide and drug overdose, however, usually lead the person into such a depressed state of consciousness that the disembodied spirit must first deal with all the unresolved elements before it is able to rejoin the oversoul fully.

Otherworldly beings

There are entities that are energies from other dimensions. There are a variety of otherworldly beings that have a connection to our world: angels, extraterrestrials, demons, and energies that come from the multiple other dimensions of existence that are far too numerous to know or mention. I do want to say here that any *benevolent* being (I would say a being of light—however, all beings are of light, perceived or not) will honor and respect you and your best interest. They will not seek to diminish, damage, disrespect, or intimidate you in any way.

Ancestral curses

Curses are words that become an energetic construct that stick to a person and then are passed down to descendants until spiritual understanding is formulated and forgiveness rendered. They can be happenstance or deliberate. An ancestral curse can be the unresolved sins or issues that are passed down to future generations who are better equipped to experience grief, find understanding, and embrace forgiveness. Forgiveness is the idea of neutrality.

Energy construct

An energy construct is the energy of the essence that is transmitted when someone speaks harsh or negative words over you. Not all harsh words turn into constructs. Constructs sometimes look like chards of glass, knives and daggers, arrows, or other jagged manifestations and can travel with the spirit into many life experiences attracting and gaining energy, volume, and momentum. Constructs can become tumors and other obstructive, diseased material in the body until they are reconciled.

Spirit guides

Everyone has a group of spirit guides, whether or not they are consciously acknowledged. I call them *my people*. Sometimes these beings are friends and family members who have died; are beings from higher or lower dimensions of energy (angels or demons); a spirit who has lived on earth or another planet and has some karmic significance; or an animal spirit or totem.

One's relationship to a spirit guide is different than a haunting. A person's ability to accept the presence of her spirit guide is unimportant to the spirit guide as it is the guide's privilege to be of service. When you have a spirit guide, it is specifically committed to you and your growth for a period of time and sometimes lifetimes. The spirit guide doesn't interfere with your life, although it can intervene in certain situations with your permission.

> When you have a spirit guide, it is specifically committed to you and your growth for a period of time and sometimes lifetimes.

I know you may be wondering, *How can a demon be my guide?* Consider that the goal in life starts at staying alive. When someone lives in a low way they need guidance on that denser path from a being with experience on it. That being can be a demon or earthbound spirit, or someone whose spirit has been willed alive again. All of these beings have vision in the lower vibrational realms.

It's important to understand that we eventually outgrow our guides and transition into new ones, based on our own growth and development. Leaving a guide behind can be as painful as moving away from your closest friend. It is a relationship out of need for a time and for a spiritual goal, and there is never the expectation that our guide will grow and mature with us as sometimes they are unable.

The guide who has helped me the most with cultivating my vision of the underworld in this life and whose vision has been invaluable, is Marie, the curandera. She is descended from a powerful *yaya nganga*, high priestess of Palo Mayumbe, and carries the burden of her vision. I'd always seen her in my mind's eye, but her image didn't become conscious for me until I was shopping at a local *botanica* (a shop for herbs, candles, and other ritual items) and saw a brand name on the package of an herbal healing bath called La Negra Curandera, The Black Healer, and it had a woman pictured very similar to the woman I saw in my mind. At that point she had been with me for about thirteen years. I'm as sure of the day she came to me as I am of the day she left. Now she visits intermittently in times of extreme grief or spiritual transition.

> The greatest tragedy is for one to have wisdom but no voice.

How I Met the Curandera: The Keeper of Secrets

I met the curandera for the first time during the holiday season of 1986. I had just begun to work for Revlon as a makeup artist and part of the special events team that worked all of the launches at Bloomingdale's and Macy's in New York City. I was about eighteen months into NYC, and after my ninth move I was a little tired, beaten down, and at the same time invigorated by my new surroundings, always thumping with the new rhythm of life. Still reeling from the trauma of being raped when I was 18, my emotions were always raw and my eyes ever vigilantly open.

I worked with quite a crew at Bloomingdale's. There was Phillip, who was a queen-sized force to be reckoned with; Kandy (at least that's what it said on her headshot); Big Mike, the jolliest teddy bear until you crossed him; and then two more gals I didn't know well as they were new. We laughed and cackled quite a bit, that group. On Tuesday afternoons on the sixth floor the promotions ran for about two weeks and all of us worked ten- to twelve-hour days. The two new girls seemed to pop up out of nowhere as was common in that business, but these girls were particularly noticeable to me because neither liked me at all, especially one of them.

Well, I have to put a disclaimer: I have no actual idea how she felt about me as I never asked, but certainly there was something in her spirit that was palpable in its hate. Every time she passed by me on her way to lunch break little daggers would fly from her eyes and venom would spill out with the words she mumbled under her breath. I know that sounds dramatic but as an empath, hate is actually a dagger that extends from someone's energy and penetrates someone who is vulnerable. Truthfully, I don't think it was her; it was just the critters that kept her company. I mean, she didn't know me at all and had no legitimate reason to dislike me other than any personal issues she may have had.

A Caribbean Queen, she was such a lovely young woman—rich, dark, cocoa skin with large, beautiful, cabled braids, and a delightfully petite round face—until of course she looked at me and the daggers flew from her eyes. At the time, I understood the demonic realms but had no words to express the common experiences that these critters promote. I understood she had visitors, but didn't understand why they sought to attack me. Every day I was so fragile, raw, and tired and then had to deal with the Caribbean Queen. Every day I felt just a little worse every time

I saw her. Finally, after much prayer and pleas for help, spirit lead me on a little journey.

I finished work early that day and headed home to my ghetto tenement flat. Just at the edge of Harlem on the West Side, I took the C train a few extra stops, and all I remember is that I was on the north side of 125th Street and walking east to the west when a spirit stopped me dead in my tracks. It was like I ran into a glass door with a counterforce that knocked me back.

Not understanding what was happening, I tried once more to walk forward and again—*bam!* It was so shocking that I started laughing uncontrollably and then looked up to realize I was standing in front of Botanica de San Miguel.

"Go in," the curandera said.

I didn't see her spirit at that time as my clairvoyance hadn't come online yet, but her presence was undeniable. I walked in and a little goat ran out from the back, followed by a man who couldn't have been a day over ninety. He spoke no English and I, in my limited Spanish, didn't get a chance to say much as it was already obvious to him what was happening to me. He walked into the back area for a brief moment and came back with his little sack of bones and shells, divining tools used in many of the African-descended religions, including Santeria.

> If we are unconscious in our awareness of the energy that we present, then we will not get the response or reaction that we expect. Getting things that we don't expect leads us to disappointment, which is a deeper level of self-awareness.

I never knew his name, but he was a santero, a priest of Santeria. Santeros throw bones and shells as a form of divination to better understand the situation they are reading. It's not the bones and shells he reads; it is the numerical pattern that comes up in throwing the bones and shells several times, leading to a corresponding spiritual dynamic between two loa, Santeria's version of saints that represent natural energy dynamics and phenomena. He made it clear he didn't need to hear me speak my broken Spanish.

We sat in silence as he threw the bones and consulted the orishas. He said a few things to me, and gave me a string of peonia seeds, a rich, fire-engine red and black seed that honors the orisha named Ellegua, the keeper of the crossroads. The only thing he said that I understood is that I was now protected. The sun had set, and as I walked home with my new set of beads and my new friend, the curandera, I wept. I felt my strength beginning to rise up in me again, with the love and support of an eternal family. Little did I know that the curandera needed me too although that was not to come for quite some time. She walked with me for the next fifteen years, sometimes in front of me, sometimes by my side, and sometimes just behind me pushing me forward and teaching me how to own myself, my life, and my choices with wisdom, grace, and silence until the time to speak would come.

The next day at Bloomingdale's, the Caribbean Queen walked past and smiled and giggled and kept on her way. We were all happier that day.

The Slayer's Altar:

Strengthening Your Spirit

The goal of this altar is to strengthen one element within yourself, such as courage, joy, integrity, or honesty. Take a few moments to consider what you think you could use more of, and remember that God gives you more courage by highlighting situations in your life for you to be courageous in.

Things You Will Need:

- An orange candle
- Something for an offering of gratitude such as a glass of water, a bowl of corn, or tobacco.
- A piece of paper with your word written on it.

Write or say a prayer with your candle in hand, tapping into the highest and best use of the element you are asking for. Being clear about asking for *the highest and best* use of your element helps you to receive whatever comes your way, as an expression of your next level of understanding. Recognize that any movement is progress and that spiritual awareness is an evolution.

PART 3
Stay Focused

Demons are smart and stupid all at the same time

The Slayer's Weapons:

Focus, Commitment, Illusion, Delusion, and Reality

The Story of the Raven

It was the first day that the chill in the morning was bearable. The warmth had come late this year. I started early and was just miles off of my destination. Almost to Crowheart, I'd gone hundreds of miles undetected. It had taken almost seven weeks. The Creator was showing me how to become invisible by becoming my environment in order to avoid being seen. I was already a skilled tracker, and learning to become invisible to others was as natural to me as breathing. Being born into generations of strife resulted in being the bearer of certain gifts. These gifts included the natural ability to fade into the side of a mountain or fly like an eagle, but my birth also had an impact that I can only see now that my heart has healed. When you are born into a way of being, and that way of being keeps you alive to see another day, it is the only way.

I was born in 1834, an emissary of the Great Spirit. I came from a long line of medicine keepers for my Navajo people. I was growing stronger in my vision and clarity; fear was becoming a thing of the past—or so I thought. The Long Walk started in the beginning of spring, 1864. Bands of my people led by the Army were taken at gunpoint and made to walk from their homelands in eastern Arizona and western New Mexico to Fort Sumner in Hwéeldi, the Pecos River valley.

Hundreds died during those eighteen days, including my entire family. The three hundred-mile relocation brought famine and disease. There was so much chaos for everyone that the entire program was abandoned just two years later…and I wasn't there for any of it. The Great Spirit had given me a vision weeks before, not of what was to come but was needed. There still was no unity among the tribes. Trust was something precarious and difficult to define. Everyone needed to survive. I was called away from my people to meet other leaders in secret. I wasn't sure who would be there, but something was coming, an enormous insult to the integrity of the heart my people. That is all I knew.

Don't misunderstand me. The land had been steeped in conflict from the time of my birth, but my righteous focus and work with the Great Spirit kept me inspired and hopeful. It was the little events and failures that nicked away at my spirit. I believed my purpose and job for my people was to heal them, yet over and over I was no match for the disease, famine, and weapons brought by the intruders. For me, the conflict was easier to handle, as I was able to preempt many things.

However, the more I saw what was coming, the less I had the ability to control it or help my loved ones; the seed of anger and resentment was planted and grew daily, every year of my life, until my rage spilled over. It was the beginning of summer, 1864, on the day I received word they had stolen my people and murdered my family. It was the day I became the raven.

I'd just arrived to meet with the other tribal leaders to discuss our mutual problem, when I was given word. Somehow the news had travelled more rapidly than me. I'd felt there was no need to travel quickly, and I'd run upon a few obstacles.

How could I have missed this? I was born and bred to not miss this?

The raven, who traveled with me and was my close companion, had been teaching me many things. How could he not have seen this? This was all wrong. I turned away from the others and ran as far and as fast as I could until I fell to my knees. The raven landed in front of me, and we sat in deafening silence for a few moments, until he spoke.

"Learning to see in the dark is different than being in darkness."

I felt so betrayed that I swung my arm out to knock him into the tree, but hadn't even noticed he'd already taken flight and was sitting on the limb above me, out of my reach.

He said, "Focusing on darkness only brings more darkness. Be careful now, or your rage will rage against you."

Turn your rage into power by focusing it on the abolition of ignorance, not of humanity. When you turn your rage on humanity it can do nothing but turn its rage back on you.

The Raven

On the way in to Crowheart, I'd passed the fort undetected. It was just yards from the meeting place. Those cowards were asleep on their feet, so many things happening just under their noses. Before I noticed my next breath, I was standing there in plain view of one of the soldiers, my arrow penetrating his forehead, then the next, then the next, then the next. I barely even had to take aim. When I was done all four soldiers at the post were dead. I exhaled. The raven was now inside of me; I could feel his wings on my arms. Together we lifted in flight...and then I awoke.

All the leaders had formed a circle around me, as I had fallen to my knees and passed out just moments before. In those few lucid moments before I became fully present in my body, the raven spoke once again: "Young man, there will be many things to rage over in your lifetime and for lifetimes to come and you have been bred to turn that rage into power not hate. Turn your rage into power by focusing it on the abolition of ignorance, not of humanity. When you turn your rage on humanity it can do nothing but turn its rage back on you. Rage ceases to be in the face of knowledge. Wisdom then becomes the new language."

The Slayer's Path: Mastering Your Emotion

Mastering your emotion is certainly a tall order and can take life times. No worries: no matter where you're starting, you'll definitely make progress. The first step is to know yourself. Learn to pay attention to the series of events that take place before you have an emotional upheaval, because they are always there if you'll notice them.

Everyone has triggers: the thoughts, memories, or beliefs that inspire anger, fear, anxiety, or grief. Your triggers may be logical, like having anxiety getting into a car because you've been in an accident; or the trigger may be illogical, like being afraid of milk. A person could have lactaphobia for many reasons that make perfect sense once you put them in perspective, but from an initial glance they don't make sense at all. Maybe as a kid you were allergic to milk or it made you really sick, but you don't remember. Maybe, in another life, you were milking a cow and it collapsed on you and you died, leaving you with a fearful and grief-stricken relationship to milk.

It has been my experience that many people with phobias have a past life or imprint explaining it perfectly, but if you don't look there, you won't find it. No matter the origin, learning to manage your deep emotions while exploring their beginnings takes time, practice, focus, and patience.

Chaos Is A Demons Playground

A demon's entire purpose is to create chaos in whatever way possible. Demons will attack any vulnerability you have, just to create a problem. Don't worry: it's their single-mindedness that leaves them ineffective. That's why they are smart and stupid all at the same time.

A demon doesn't necessarily attack you directly. Sometimes they influence the gray area of your thoughts (illusions), emotions (delusions), or choices (realities). They can add subtle influence to your own self-deprecating thoughts or get you to play the *assuming makes an ass out of u+me* game: assuming you know what a person is thinking or intending and reacting because of it.

If you don't know what your normal is, demons can be successful in their influence, weighting your already-sensitive emotions with the last straw, exacerbating your anger, anxiety, grief, fear, or other emotions. There are demons whose sole purpose is to amplify whatever you are feeling.

> Delusion is the experiential phase of your creative process, where the intent or interpretation of an idea is dense, so thick you can cut it with a knife. It will feel as if energetic things are real or happening and may be experienced by most senses as emotionally and energetically tangible.

Did you know that the word *illusion* comes from the Latin word *ludere*? It means to play or to frolic. Hmmm...so when you are experiencing illusions, you are *playing* and *frolicking* in your mind or creating your own personal universe.

Understanding the concepts of illusion, delusion, and reality is important. In psychiatry, delusion is considered a pathology and is related to mental illness. In different spiritual traditions, such as Hinduism or Buddhism, delusion is considered to be the essence that keeps us from realization of the true nature of all things. The concept is tricky because in an emotional, fearful lens it is easy to be mistaken and experience delusion as being inappropriate, bad, or wrong—something to stop or overcome.

For instance, you don't want to have a delusive epiphany that you can fly and then try to jump off a building because of that delusion. Our negative judgments about delusions are a product of our human habit of linear thinking, which is set up to keep us living every minute possible.

The Slayer's Path: **Mastering Your Emotion**

So this is what I would like to do. Relate to delusion as a natural part of our creative process, which allows us to be able to visualize with a particular level of density, prior to making choices that make the presence of that delusion impact the real physical world through our choices. For my intents and purposes here, delusions are our creative manifestations that range from carrying the dead to the creative process of strategy.

Similarly, illusion is a natural part of our creative process. The process of density moves from illusion (idea state), to delusion (idea with essence), to reality (the physical result of choices made). Illusion is the mind's first connection to the intent or interpretation of the self.

Delusion is the experiential phase of your creative process, where the intent or interpretation is much more energetically dense in nature and may be experienced by most senses as being real and emotionally and energetically tangible, like a vision or mirage. That vision is real within the realm that it exists, but may take very specific criteria in order to become manifest in the physical world.

Reality is defined here as the physical realm, where we can see what illusions and delusions can be brought into manifestation or not. The idea of truth on a human level is what can be brought into physical manifestation, and the spiritual idea of truth is that there is absolutely no separation between us and the Creator. It is illusion, delusion, and reality that fill the gap between the two concepts of truth.

THE PROCESS OF THINKING, THE KAHUNAS BELIEVED, CREATES THOUGHT FORMS. AND, AS MOST THOUGHTS COME IN A TRAIN AND IN RELATION TO OTHER THOUGHTS, THE SHADOWY BODIES OF THOUGHTS (THOUGHT FORMS) GROUP IN CLUSTERS.
BRAD STEIGER, *KAHUNA MAGIC*

The Purpose of Emotion and its Impact on Perception

Illusion is the first step of the creative process; we can also call it *imagination*. When you begin with a new concept or idea, the next phase in the processing of that idea occurs when your spirit determines the purpose and the possibility of manifesting that idea.

Max Freedom Long's writings on Huna explains this concept well by breaking down the way *the self* processes information into three aspects: the low, the middle, and the higher self (and the way they communicate). When a new idea enters the system through the higher self, it is first sent to the low self (connected to the emotions) to determine any obstacles to its creation. Based on the information accessed there, the middle self (connected to the body and worldly implementation) can go to work.

Let's put a picture to this: say you want to be in a romantic relationship. You meet your dream mate, and you go on a few dates. The next natural response is to begin to go over in your mind all the reasons why he or she isn't good enough. Have you ever done that? To do that is the natural way that we process our fitness for the goal we have in mind and zero in on the details of the object of our inquiry.

What does it look like when a demon attacks your imagination?

Now, if you're experiencing demonic attack, that same process can be exacerbated and intensified. Whether you are having intensely negative thoughts, or blindingly positive thoughts, either way, the process is not completely rational and does not match the factual information available. Remember, a demon wants to create chaos—period. This chaos could be created by, say, having you get into a situation that brings you discord and unhappiness, or maybe by keeping you from the very thing that will bring you joy.

What does it look like when a demon attacks your visions?

Delusions are the images of illusion with essence; we can also call them visions. For a period of about six months in my life I kept having visions of hitting someone with my car. Of course, I had no interest in that, but the thought and vision kept haunting me, and in fact, I had three solid opportunities to engage in some sort of accident and was able to avert each one. I prayed every time I got in the car that I would not hit anyone and that they would not hit me. It was the most difficult driving at night because my clairvoyance had just really opened up. I wasn't quite used to it and at night especially I always saw folks (spirits) in the street. I can't tell you how many times I stopped flat in the middle of the road because I saw a guy walking but he wasn't physically really there.

Sheepishly, I'd wave at the other motorists like, *Ya, I'm okay. Nothing to see here...I'm driving on now.* And with a little wave, I'd push on down the road. My heart would beat so fast every time that would happen. It got so bad that I just wouldn't drive at night anymore, and when I had to go out to the grocery or the bank, I'd try to go between five and seven in the morning when there weren't too many real people out.

The other element of it was the fear. I was under demonic attack quite a bit at the time, and my fear would be amplified tenfold. Although I was clear that hitting and hurting someone was not an option for me, I thought about it a lot, and it created an enormous amount of anxiety. The first opportunity came when I was on a busy street where all four directions of the intersection were backed up. I had the green light and was moving slowly through the intersection when I noticed that the guy opposite me in the left turning lane just didn't seem right. I had just headed into the intersection, and he began to turn left. As the traffic was back-to-back, this just wasn't a rational decision on his part; there really was nowhere for him to go other than to plow right into me.

I pressed incessantly on the horn and said out loud, "Stop it! Do not move forward!"

That seemed, for a brief moment, to stop his momentum, and then just as I passed out of his range of motion, he continued on with his left turn and completely nailed the girl in the Honda in back of me, spinning both of them in opposite directions across the intersection.

I was in awe. I got through the light and pulled over to the right to see if the girl was okay. Her car had spun out and crashed into a fence, deploying the airbags. I felt so bad, because it definitely could have been me. The man, however, didn't make it. He spun out and crashed into a pole. I believe he may have had a heart attack. I only saw the fire department drive away with his lifeless body. I stayed firmly planted with the girl in the Honda for several hours until her family could come get her; the car was totaled, but luckily there wasn't a scratch on her.

After that, I was even more hyper-vigilant. The fear was as thick as concrete, and I would feel sick to my stomach when I had to go out into the world with my car. It was a very unique experience. Part of me felt safe and certain that I would not hurt anyone or be hurt myself. The same part of me that felt peaceful and aware of my surroundings at all times was safe in my command of my world.

Then there was the other half of the experience, the part where I felt anxious and fearful all of the time, the part of myself that the demons around me could influence with their continual barrage of doubt. Would I miss a beat, a sign, an event? Will something bad happen if I don't pay attention to that the guy crossing the street? All that I could do at the time was reaffirm to myself over and over that it just was not going to happen. *It wasn't an option.*

Then came the second test of my faith: Pulling slowly out of a driveway from the bank, crossing the sidewalk to pull out onto the street, I saw a man on a bike about ten feet away. He literally began to ride towards me from a total stop, running directly into the side of my vehicle, and wobbling on his bike around to the front of the car, he just fell over.

Again, this did not make any sense. It was like a ridiculous, slow-motion dream, but yet it was completely happening. There is no way any of this was logical. It became clear that this guy was up to no good, looking to get insurance money.

Hmmm, I thought, *I am not sure what to do here.*

I put my car in park, got out of the car, and came around to where he was on the ground and asked if he was okay. The voice in my head said to call an ambulance.

He said, "Ya, I'm fine."

I said, "Do you want me to call an ambulance?"

"No, I'm fine."

Again, the voice in my head said, *Call an ambulance.* "You know, I'm going to go ahead and call the ambulance. I need to know that you are okay."

Helping him over to a chair near the attendant in the parking lot, we waited there for the emergency people. He was fine and refused to go to the hospital for X-rays. After we exchanged information he went on his way. The firefighter told me that he was certain the guy was looking for a payout. He said it was right for me to call the paramedics; the fact that he didn't need and refused service eliminated any possibility for him to sue me. My insurance paid for the paramedics and that was about it. And wouldn't you know it, the guy came back and told the parking lot attendant how mad he was that he didn't get his payout. Strike two averted.

The final time was early on an October morning. It must've been about seven a.m. or so. As I drove down the main street near where I lived there was no traffic yet, but I noticed that my foot was beginning to press on the brake. I was just coming around the bend where there was going to be a light in about a hundred feet, but I couldn't yet see it. I slowed almost to a complete stop just as I saw the intersection. There was a police officer directing traffic, and just over to his left in the middle of the intersection was a person covered completely in a sheet. My gaze met the officer's as I was passing through, and just after passing him I burst into tears. I cried all the way to my next destination. I knew then that it was over. The man lying dead in the road was hit by someone else. I prayed for him, his loved ones, and the officer that night. I never worried about hitting anyone again after that.

Delusion and Weighted Emotion

The remedy in distinguishing weighted emotion is to be honest about your feelings and learn to express them in a productive way. I worked with a client, Marissa, a young business executive; she was a stunning, charming young lady who had a tremendous amount of anger. So much in fact, that almost everything triggered her.

The most important thing to know about angry people is that they are not just angry. Anger emerges out of a person's desire to heal pain. The expression of anger lifts you up out of the pain element and transforms the pain into a new energy; the intensity of the anger is directly based on the density of the pain it is transforming. So if you are deeply entrenched in pain, anger will be moved into rage; hurt feelings will be moved into irritability; and so on.

Through our work we discovered that her lowest common denominator was feeling like she was a burden to everyone. Because she felt like a burden, she didn't feel pretty enough, smart enough, funny enough, happy enough, powerful enough, valuable enough, and so many other not enoughs. Almost anything anyone said to her felt like an insult. The minute she felt insulted on the outside, she would remember the burden she felt on the inside and fly into a rage, oftentimes not remembering anything that she said or did while raging. As this dynamic began to break down all of the relationships in her life, she became more angry and confused. In our work we began to trace back where she felt weighted emotion.

Weighted emotion occurs when the amount of feeling—anger, grief, anxiety, or fear—is not rational for the situation or memory. A rational amount of emotion is the amount of emotion that you would expect in the situation or in reliving the memory. It is not what others would expect for you, or what they would feel, but what you would expect to feel. We have a natural emotional barometer within us that lets us know intuitively when our emotions are weighted by other influences, sometimes by other people and their feelings, or by layers of trauma and unexpressed emotion from this or a past life, or sometimes by otherworldly influences.

Marissa became aware of a past life she'd lived in western America in the 1800s during a drought. Food was scarce, and there wasn't enough food to feed all the mouths in the family, leaving her with the feeling of being a burden. In this life, she had an eating disorder in addition to many other health problems and conflicted relationships with both of her parents. All of those things, coupled with a demonic energy that haunted her, left her vulnerable and emotionally weighted.

As we reconciled and cleared the burdensome past life, she found it easier to manage her relationship to food, and it became clear for her that much of her burden stigma was not related to her parents, therefore allowing her to change her dynamic with them. All of this lessening the weight of her emotion allowed her to recognize when she was being visited and spoken to by the demon haunting her, rendering her more empowered in the situation. As she balanced out emotionally, and as the grief from those things had been processed, the demon could have no more impact.

> Grief is like a two hundred-pound bag of rice; with every emotional expression of grief, a bowl of rice is cooked and eaten. Once the rice is gone...the rice is gone.

Unexpressed Emotion Travels

While we can carry any kind of sentiment with us into other lives or other experiences, the denser emotions such as fear, rage, and grief can multiply over time and space to create what may exist today as an entity. The seven deadly sins are a perfect model to use in order to understand the origin of the entities that we call demons. The energy of wrath, greed, sloth, pride, lust, envy, and gluttony can manifest as creatures of a person's perception of those energies.

One time, at the beginning of my career, I had an interaction with a neighbor who understood that I made my living as a spiritualist. For him, that understanding was very limited. I got up one morning and as I took my morning laps around the complex, I saw him giving me the major stare-down as he stood by the fence with a cup of coffee. The intensity of the stare caught my eye and as I tuned in I knew it wasn't him at all. It was a critter that was attached to him.

Gary was a docile pothead who stayed up all night playing music and hanging with his friends. At least that is what I had seen of him so far. The look through his eyes on this morning was not that at all. On about my third lap, I decided that it would be important to confront whatever this thing was, sooner rather than later.

On the fourth lap, seeing his vicious stare-down, I walked up to him and said, "So...do you have something to say to me?"

His response came hard, quick, and a little incoherent. "I know what you are. You are a psychic, witch, and tarot [he pronounced it tear-rot] card reader that steals social security checks from old ladies."

He rattled on with a few other vulgar statements about who I was, and as he was angrily jabbering on, I started to feel the sensation of my spirit drawing on the power of the universe. This sensation rose up in me as if from the core of the Earth. My heart opened, I raised my hand, and I pointed at him, as if to direct the energy of my sentiment.

"You…will not…fuck…with me." I enunciated each word slowly and deliberately in a firm and even tone.

It seemed as if it may have been heard by no one else but him, as if to others watching the exchange it was just a regular conversation. I then drew that energy back and turned away from him on my heel with a little bounce in my step and a chuckle so large that I had to hold onto it as I moved out of earshot, going back to my apartment just a few doors down.

My chuckle turned into an enormous feeling of joy as I sat in my apartment and wondered, *What the hell just happened?* In what felt like an hour, the information came that there was an entity that he had been carrying a long time that protected him from revelation. I also got that his spirit had been desiring to release the entity for a while, but that his daily pot smoking kept it concealed for the most part.

As I was having this conversation with his spirit in my head about ten minutes later, I heard a valiant knock on the door. It was Gary. He immediately apologized. He said we had gotten off on the wrong foot and asked if we could talk for a minute. I invited him in, and he sat on the couch across from me.

During our conversation, which actually lasted about an hour, I witnessed a few different things going on. He did most of the talking and would go from saying nice and kind things, to calling me a neophyte and letting me know that he was sure I was beneath him. It was really fascinating. I knew that the entity I had encountered was still there, and that the man was trying his best to keep him at bay. I wondered, what exactly he was looking to get rid of, if it wasn't the critter he was battling with. Soon he left and I sat on the couch, not really even noticing how tired I was. It was at least another couple of hours when my phone rang.

It was one of my psychic colleagues. I was too tired to answer and let the machine pick up.

At that time it was an actual answering machine, and I heard her message loud and clear: *Tracee, are you ok? What's going on over there? Something is in your apartment. Call me back.*

In that moment, I understood. I closed my eyes and felt the enormity of the weight on me. Just in my acknowledgement of its presence, it began to lift from me. As it lifted, I saw it as a big blob of dirty-green energy. It had a smile on its face as it floated further and further away from me; it actually smiled, waved, and danced away, as if to say, *Thanks for the help.*

I then called on St. Michael to assist the critter in being transformed into usable energy for the universe. I find it best to be thorough. Now my awareness came back to the couch and to my body lying on it. I felt lighter and now completely awake and joyful. I called my friend to say thanks for paying attention for me, and all was well.

As I sat and reflected on the experience and on the nature of the critter, the dominant energy was closest to that of gluttony, the kind of weariness and apathy that sets in after you've eaten a huge meal multiplied by a thousand. It was like several wet blankets that were just warm enough to be tolerable and heavy enough to make you lose all interest in pushing them off of you. After I acknowledged the nature of the energy and after it had been released, I lost sight of it completely. My work was done and my relationship to my neighbor went back to being neutral as if we hadn't had any interaction at all.

Becoming Psychic

When you experience your first quantum shift into awareness on other levels, it is easy to become a know-it-all. Your first experiences are about learning to read situations and yourself, and learning to trust your instincts. However, remember that all of your experiences are not about what you know about others through the process; it is what you learn about yourself.

When you receive an insight about someone, always ask their permission before you share the insight with them. It is not your job to enlighten them; it just may be your job to keep their secret. If they want to know and you tell them, be aware of their response. Any resistance to the information is not denial on their part, nor are you wrong but somewhere in between.

Remember, the experience is happening so that you can learn about yourself. Resistance is an indicator that the information is seeking to open up and expand *your* beliefs and vision, not those of the other person. When you get caught up in making it about the other person, you lose perspective and you miss the point. Staying focused on your self-knowledge is the shortest distance between A and B.

> The Raven's spiritual meaning is one of the void, a place in between, where time isn't linear and unresolved past experiences live boldly with the present and create the future, a place where integrity, authenticity, and accountability are kings. A totem deserving of apparent awe, the raven represents the Creator himself.

Telepathic Communication—The Watcher

Telepathy is the dominant way of communication, whether or not you are aware of it. We have spoken volumes long before any verbal conversation takes place. As you become consciously aware of this fact, your head can get pretty crowded. We have a long-running joke, my sister and I. We had gone for coffee one day at a very colorful café. I mean the customers. Quite a few students, business folk, homeless, and some criminals, I am sure. Everybody drinks coffee. As we were standing in line, a man who seemed to be in his sixties and had apparently not showered for days, walked past me.

As he was talking with one of the entourage in his head, he said, "Christina Aguilera is my girlfriend." And then he looked at me and said (as he pointed to his forehead with two fingers on his right hand), "She's going to call me later."

Oh my, creation above--we laughed so hard we cried. And as we parted that day we did the two fingers to the forehead, "I'll call to you later."

Who knew that phrase would become such an integral part of my life? When my mother took ill, I would say to her, "Hey, Mom, I'll call [two fingers to the forehead] later," and she would just laugh. In her last few months, she was in the hospital for a few weeks. She had begun to go in and out of the physical world in her spiritual awareness. When I would leave to go back home or sometimes just leave the room, she would say, "Hey Trace, I'll call you later."

Her spiritual awareness expanded to the point where she often thought I was in town or in the room, when I was actually in LA thinking about her and talking to her in my head. I am so grateful for that guy at the coffee shop. I tell him that all the time.

Discernment is key

When your attention is focused in the physical world, your energy body is still open to receive messages. So when you see that crazy homeless person on the street, he is not crazier than you; he just has an awareness of all the information coming in and is in the process of learning how to assimilate and interpret it. Some people already know how to do this and some people do not. This is why knowing yourself and your imprints is so important: being able to discern your energy from that of another allows you not to be moved by it.

For example, you could be standing behind the angry guy in the checkout line and then all of a sudden get irritable because the line is not moving fast enough. When you recognize that you didn't walk in mad and that you have plenty of time, you are able to let go of the anger before you claim it and react because of it. Understanding that this is the way it works also helps in empowering you to respond in all kinds of situations.

Your vibe is very powerful

One day in mid-morning, I was pulling out of Carl's Jr. and was the first person to stop at the red light. A little, reddish-colored sedan with a teenage boy driving was waiting in the left-turn lane, with the green light, adjacent to me. Behind him pulled an older truck, also reddish, driven by a thirty-something man. All of a sudden the man in the truck, who was at a full stop, got out of his vehicle and hurled a full, unopened can of Coca-Cola at the young man's car. At this precise moment, the young man's lane became clear and he peeled out, made his left turn, stopped about twenty feet past me, and in a rage flung himself out of the car. He looked up in a fury and then dove into the back seat of his car, as if to get something. I was certain he was going to pull out a gun.

Now, keep in mind that I am situated right in the line of their conflict's fire. Even the two people standing on the corner of the street automatically ducked for the barrage of bullets at the guy in the red truck we all felt was to come. In a split second, as I was looking at this young man from my left side-view mirror, I decided I had no interest in being a casualty. I began to speak to this young man, caught in the throes of his anger, in my mind.

I said to him, *You do not have to do this. It is not worth it. You have people in your life that love and care about you. At best you'll go to jail, at worst someone will die. I love you!*

At that moment the young man emerged from his backseat looking confused, as if someone stole his thoughts and he didn't remember what he was doing. He stood there for a minute, and then got back into his car and drove away. The other idiot in the truck luckily had to wait for the next light. I made a right and drove aimlessly for about ten minutes while I cried it out. I am sure we dodged a bullet that day. Literally.

> When you have a strong belief about anything, trying to change it can really be frustrating. Know that there is a natural sense of loyalty one has to their beliefs, as well as a sense of betrayal in some way (to yourself and others) if you change them. Remember, grief is a part of any transition, but letting go of the old worn out belief and embracing a new one...always leads to more; joy, love, and acceptance. Just more.

The Slayer's Motto: I Am Not Defined by My World

All her life, Shelley tried to do bigger and better than before, to *be* bigger and better than before. But no matter how hard she tried, nothing ever felt good enough. She seemed to provoke disappointment and criticism from many who knew her. One day, in utter futility, she realized she couldn't live with the burden of being a disappointment anymore. Being a burden was no longer an option. After a bit of spiritual exploration, she realized that the issue wasn't how she did things, or the level of her success or impact on others. The issue was that she was disappointed in herself and expected to disappoint others. How could she ever be satisfied with anything while unconsciously believing that anything that she did, wasn't good enough? This was the epiphany that opened her to the real work. Why did she always feel like a burden?

The Slayer's Motto:
I Am Not Defined by My World

Imprisoned by your beliefs

Spiritually, our soul comes equipped with different thoughts and beliefs from our spiritual history, and our DNA is imprinted with our ancestral history. After we're born, we are imprinted with the beliefs, values, and ideals from our environment, family, and friends. It is the harmony or conflict of these beliefs that shapes who we are, that can either protect us or make us vulnerable to the Devil.

AS MAN ADVANCES IN CIVILIZATION, AND SMALL TRIBES ARE UNITED INTO LARGER COMMUNITIES, THE SIMPLEST REASON WOULD TELL EACH INDIVIDUAL THAT HE OUGHT TO EXTEND HIS SOCIAL INSTINCTS AND SYMPATHIES TO ALL THE MEMBERS OF THE SAME NATION, THOUGH PERSONALLY UNKNOWN TO HIM. THIS POINT BEING ONCE REACHED, THERE IS ONLY AN ARTIFICIAL BARRIER TO PREVENT HIS SYMPATHIES EXTENDING TO THE MEN OF ALL NATIONS AND RACES.
CHARLES DARWIN

The Slayer's Pact: Heal Yourself

Healing yourself can be a life-long pursuit. What does it look like to be healed? What does it feel like to be healed? Emotionally, do you still feel anger, anxiety, and grief when you are healed? Well, in a nutshell, being healed really means no longer being triggered by, or being attached to holding on to or repressing, your deep emotion. Feeling is the way you connect to yourself, the world, and the Creator. Feeling is something you will always be able to do. The goal is to experience what you feel fully, without letting your feelings dictate the show.

Daily battles of a slayer

Even everyday situations can go awry. A decision that every single one of us will make periodically, if not daily, is whether to get involved in a situation that doesn't really appear to include us. It leads us to two questions: At what point or under what circumstance do we change how we see being included in situations that we may witness or happen upon? And when do we start to challenge our fear-based ideas about being involved?

In my philosophy, if I see, hear, or witness, I am included. Is there a possibility that instead of running in fear from each other, that we look at each other in compassion and encourage and require more from one another? And in friendship, do you tell what you know? Can you support your friendships without taking sides? They say that when you know better, you do better. So is it too much to ask that we be willing to risk educating each other to do better?

The Slayer's Pact: **Heal Yourself**

Several years ago I ended up in a common dilemma. My boyfriend was having sex with many other women and lying about it. I found out by receiving a text-messaged picture of his genitals from his latest conquest. As disheartening as it was, I'd suspected it and prayed every night for the unequivocal truth until it came. And the truth was partially erect and absolutely unequivocal.

Now for a little backstory: As it turned out, one of my friends and longtime colleagues knew my boyfriend and they'd been friends since childhood. My colleague had said over and over how lucky his friend was to have me in his life. After the incident, I struggled and struggled with telling him. We'd had a fairly close relationship and many conversations about personal matters in the past. I figured he would eventually ask about him and our relationship. Finally, the day and the dialogue came.

Much to my inner resistance, I told him the highlights of the story. And what came next was a bit of a surprise. Feeling the awkward silence of regret, I said, "Should I not have told you?"

His response was, "Well, it is what it is. I'm not going to take sides either way."

Interestingly enough, these few words were more heartbreaking to me than that text message. I wasn't looking for him to take sides. I mean, really, how can one take a side in this circumstance? I think it was the tone in his voice and what appeared to be the lack of caring and compassion. Or was it the cold chill that came over him as he said it? Or was it my illusion of the person I thought I knew? All of these questions were running on the crawl in my mind. Then came more questions: What should he have said? His loyalty clearly went to his friend…or did it? Because he presents himself as a loving, compassionate person who cares for me as a friend, should he have displayed that in this situation? He seemed to have an opinion about the situation before this?

And furthermore, should he have said, "I am sorry my friend is such a jerk"?

Can you show compassion and caring without the appearance of taking sides?

Wow, the crawl in my mind was busy.

> Do you know that life is not always like that? That, philosophically speaking, when you cut in front of others, others will eventually cut in front of you? That many little things will turn into one big thing? That you reap what you sow?

Every day, we have the opportunity to give a little extra to each other, and we don't because we don't believe we have the time, the resources, the skill, or the heart. Or simply the illusion that showing compassion is the same as agreement or alliance. And what about my responsibility? Should I have listened to my instinct not to tell him, to save me from further disappointment? I mean, do buddies want to know these things about each other? And furthermore, how could he not know how his friend is?

Should I have told him how I felt about his response? Or did everything happen perfectly so that you and I could be having this conversation? I really wanted some wisdom here.

And in a few days it came. Standing in the eternal security line at the airport, I was about fifty feet from where the line began when a young man walked up and cut in front of me. He couldn't have been more than nineteen and was a bit imposing, standing about six feet three inches, weighing three hundred pounds, and bearing at least five tattoos that I could see.

In amazement I glared at him, and he said, "How you doing?"

I said, "Good, How are *you* doing?" in awe of his audacity.

Then I thought of my situation, and that if no one ever says anything, how is the world going to change? I looked at the young man, and the crawl started. *What should I do? Should I tell him that the line ends over there? No, he looked a bit puffed up as if to say, I'll go off if you say something. Or was that just his tattoos or my insecurity speaking?*

I didn't really feel fearful of him—he was wearing a bright purple shirt for God's sake. *I mean, do violent people wear purple? Does he already know where the line begins? Of course he knows.*

Oh my, this was turning into quite a dilemma in my mind. I didn't want to be one of those people who doesn't care and does nothing.

So I stopped the crawl and quieted my mind. I said nothing but stayed close as we navigated the line together. He looked at me a couple of times in irritation of my penetrating gaze. I asked myself what was at the bottom of this pile. Was it really that he cut in front of me? No, it was his illusion that taking advantage of people and situations because you can made him powerful. Is *that* what it was? So, now that I had his undivided telepathic attention, I had a few questions.

Do you know that life is not always like that? That, philosophically speaking, when you cut in front of others, others will eventually cut in front of you? That many little things will turn into one big thing? That you reap what you sow…

Man, I was a little fired up. As we moved into the building where there were many security officers, I revisited the idea of actually saying something to him, and then I noticed his ticket. His name was Jared. He had an old-school ticket, so clearly he wasn't a frequent flyer. Maybe he really didn't know where the line started. What if I said something rudely, and it made him feel bad. At this realization, all of a sudden I felt calm. Clearly it was important for me to truly consider him too; otherwise, I suppose I'd be like him. My heart felt peaceful. I also felt content about my telepathic words to Jared's mind, and will hold that intent for him until he's ready to hear it in the real world. What a ridiculously profound journey that was for me.

To be a slayer or a watcher

A dilemma I think everyone has encountered at least once in their lives is whether or not to enter into a situation that you're not really a part of, concerning someone you care about. There have been a couple of experiences in my life with girlfriends and their boyfriends, where the boyfriend made an overtly inappropriate overture towards me, and I turned him down flat.

In both incidents alcohol was involved, and when I went to both friends to say, "Hey look, I'm sorry, but your guy came on to me last night," both of the ladies responded the same way: thanking me for saying something, apologizing for their man, and then no longer speaking to me.

It's always a crapshoot how someone will respond in that situation, but for me, there is no other action to take but to divulge the truth and let everything shake out as it may. I really appreciated being told the truth. Now I think I would have preferred a phone call instead of a dick-pic, but I did ask for no ambiguity.

No matter where you stand on this, I will hold the space for you to have the time to make the effort, to have the resources of courage and wisdom to participate, and to develop the skill of confidence to know not only that you are doing whatever the right thing is, but also to know that you will not suffer for it. At the very least, hold the intent of truth for yourself or someone else. Maybe this way the world will change.

THE CREATION SPEAKETH A UNIVERSAL LANGUAGE, INDEPENDENTLY OF HUMAN SPEECH OR HUMAN LANGUAGE, MULTIPLIED AND VARIOUS AS THEY BE. IT IS AN EVER EXISTING ORIGINAL, WHICH EVERY MAN CAN READ. IT CANNOT BE FORGED; IT CANNOT BE COUNTERFEITED; IT CANNOT BE LOST; IT CANNOT BE ALTERED; IT CANNOT BE SUPPRESSED.

THOMAS PAINE

Jurisdiction: Take Care of Your Own

Just as a rock hits the water, it creates an irrevocable ripple. No matter what, the water cannot be unmoved. That's what happens when we make a choice. Choice is a phase of the creative process in which some sort of decision is made or action taken that makes a significant, irrevocable change. Although any decision that's made can be changed, you can never unknow what you've learned from the process. Although all the effects of those choices can be compensated for by other choices, we can never undo what has been done. That is the definition of karma. It knows no time and space. The reactions to the actions remain until they are neutralized, or brought into balance through new actions. Your ability to choose, then, becomes the most important asset you have. Even in situations in which it may appear that you have no choice, you always have the choice of how you will find acceptance of the situation.

Surrender is closely connected to choice, because if you haven't accepted the current situation, then that means you're not in present time. Living in the now is one of the few fun little buzzwords that you hear a lot these days. However, that little word *now* packs a wallop. If you are not present to your situation, then you are processing the past, or preparing for the future. Both processing the past and preparing for the future are very important parts of the process that lays the foundation for choice. For example, *packing* for your vacation is not *going* on your vacation.

Don't worry: It's just your imagination

Demons can capitalize the most on your creative process as it is closest to their dimension. They capitalize by amplifying your fear and negative thinking and sometimes by embellishing it to the point that your fears seem to manifest. There are specific demons for whom this is the only activity in which they engage. This is the reason it is paramount to understand and know your strengths and vulnerabilities and to be clear on the path of the creative process. It is no wonder artists throughout history have personified the Devil and demon battle with their art. Those wily bastards desperately don't want you to think clearly, express your truth, or feel love in any way…if they can help it.

I have always had an active imagination. Anything I have ever done, I spent hours on it in my mind first. It would appear that my personality dictates that I am impetuous and impulsive, but in fact I am not. The countless hours of daydreaming are now called *visioning* as I am a mature professional. But really, it's just daydreaming, sorting out every detail of an action and its consequences, or every word in a conversation, in order to fully recognize my full meaning and intention so as to own every ripple I make.

Daydreaming has even been the way I stay prepared for the world that I live in, picturing myself cleaning my house, dancing without care, and even warding off evil with complete and unequivocal success. It has also been the way I am able to tolerate witnessing for someone some of the most unimaginable sufferings that this world has to offer. My inner crime fighter is a combination of Storm, Wonder Woman, and Bruce Lee. I always loved the way Wonder Woman stopped a speeding bullet, or how Storm changed the entire environment with a little focus and arm swinging. Somehow I have always seen that as possible.

Obviously, imagining having a better life is not necessarily a new theme, but a recent trip and fall triggered a reflection on how many times my meanderings of the mind have prepared me to be safe, sane, courageous, physically adept, and joyful in the physical world.

Stop, drop, and roll in my mind

The other day, as I walked down the street to meet a friend at the local café, I tripped. Plunging forward, somehow I caught myself and kept walking. The trip made me realize that I forgot something at home, so I turned back. I tripped again in the exact same spot. This time I was going down. In that split second of falling I thought to myself, *I will not be hurt by this.*

My shoulder automatically turned in and I tucked and rolled. If there had been a little more momentum, then I would have landed on my feet again.

There I lay in the middle of the sidewalk in a little ball, without even a scratch, laughing. I easily got up, and surprisingly nothing was hurt. As I walked to the café, my heart swelled with joy.

You see, I spend a lot of time wondering what I would do if I had to get out of the way of a speeding car, escape from a burning building, or fend off an attacker. So, I often visualize the dive and roll, or the round-house kick to the jaw. I imagine that my legs are strong and my form is impeccable. Of course, I don't spend all day on these things, but several times a day I catch myself in little, thirty-second snippets questioning what I would do if this or that happened. I always visualize the answer, and that day I had proof that it is not time wasted.

Hip-hop in my mind

I love to dance. I went to NYC and dancing was to be a part of my repertoire. I quickly learned that I was more of a choreographer than a dancer, and I definitely was not an athlete. I held so much emotion in my gut, and those feelings always found a way to come pouring out. That's workable for yoga class, but definitely not for ballet or even jazz.

I planted myself firmly into Afro-Haitian dance where I was free to dance and feel in the way I needed. The thing that I got from dance was learning to move with the flow of the universe, bending, weaving, and being a conduit for the universal life force. Thinking in this way brought to me an ultra-awareness of the subtle influx of change and how to move with it instead of against it; how to move towards the steps I could do, and do them well, always seeing myself becoming good at the things I wasn't good at just yet.

Hip-hop dance was just blooming at the time, and I was awful at it. You really need great balance to be good at hip-hop, and imbalance is my specialty. However, in my mind, I am amazing. I can even do flips; get up with one leg, no hands; and the ol' slide and spin. I always feel invigorated after a thirty-second hip-hop session in my mind.

I want to throw in here that many of us spend hours of time per week imagining awful things happening or fearfully visualizing the exact outcome we don't want. It is a part of our mental nature to replay, over and over in our mind, a distasteful or traumatic experience we had or fear having. Add that to some human's extraordinary skill at telepathy and you could have a situation in which a tidal wave of unwanted thoughts and then feelings that aren't yet real—or even yours for that matter—begin to manifest.

> The thing that I got from dance was learning to move with the flow of the universe, bending, weaving, and being a conduit for the universal life force.

That brings me to another real-world application. I was at the doctor's office one morning, and walking out the door just before me was a lady who was clearly on her last appointment before the baby came. Her husband was about twenty feet away talking to reception when I opened the door for her and motioned her to go before me.

She smiled and softly said, "Thank you."

Something was not right in her voice. Without thinking about it, my body began to drop to one knee about the same time that I realized that she was going to pass out. It was only a few seconds before I had the full weight of her sitting on the impromptu chair I had created with my knee. Her husband noticed at the point her head fell back on my shoulder. She was out.

He and the nurse came running over and we shared an awkward glance, as if to say, *Is this your pregnant wife on my lap?* She came to. They got her some juice and helped her to a real chair.

The husband said, "Thanks."

I replied, "No problem," and walked out the door and moved on with the day. As I laughed to my car, I thought, "I really love hip-hop."

Bruce lee in my mind

I had a poster of Bruce Lee in my room literally all my childhood. I always felt a special connection to him and to the martial arts. The concept of using an opponent's energy against her, or summoning and directing universal chi, always resonated with me. However, like I said, I am only an athlete in my mind. So when I took those six months of jujitsu, it was a bit of a struggle. Sparring just for the sake of sparring did not make sense to me. My kung fu was definitely magical like the old Chinese martial arts movies. Flying through the air for a triple running kick—now how could that possibly help me in my future? Well, I found that warding off evil began with making some personal decisions: (1) deciding you're not going to be a victim; (2) deciding that you will not be around violence or that violence cannot be within or around you; and (3) knowing that the universal life force flows through you and you can align with it.

One Sunday evening around dusk, as I was walking down an old cobblestone street on the Lower East Side of NYC, I saw these two gentlemen walking on the other side of the street; they were eyeing me and I knew they weren't gentlemen at all. Even though it was still early, the street was vacant and quiet. I needed to cross to their side of the street to get to the train, so just as they passed, I crossed diagonally to end up behind them on the same sidewalk.

Just as I stepped into the street, so did they. They were causing me to directly confront them. Knowing that the meeting was inevitable, I said, in my mind, *I will not have this. Whatever this is, I will not have it.* Just as we crossed paths in the center of the street, the taller gentleman began to take something from the inside of his jacket. He raised his arm up above his head. With a clinched fist, the back of his hand was about to come down on me.

I raised two fingers to him, and said, "Uh uh," as I shook my head.

He and his friend were so befuddled by this that he mimicked me, in a fairly high tone for a man, saying, "Uh uh," and sort of waived his hands in confusion.

I just kept going and did not look back. When I got to the next block I broke down in tears and cried and laughed all the way home. As it turns out, the two-fingered hand position I gave him happened to be called the *prana mudra*, a yoga hand position that strengthens life force. It certainly did that night.

Day dreaming: more than it's cracked up to be

Watching the evening news can be tumultuous, for some. Just getting through the day without worry in this sometimes desperate place that we all share is a feat. So I recommend that once a day in your quiet time, you answer one version of the question, "What would I do if...?" And since it is your vision, it can only end well for everyone. You never know when it will come in handy.

You make the choice; the creator makes the change

Processing the past includes ignorance, resistance, conflict, and surrender. That is seeing yourself through others' eyes, becoming aware of yourself, weighing the pros and cons of who you are, and finally accepting them as they are. When you have arrived at a place where you simply accept what you are or how you are in the moment, then you can decide to continue in that way or make a choice that creates change.

When your consciousness is completely focused in the moment that is when you enlist the assistance of the Creator to obtain a physical result. Don't get me wrong: the Creator is involved with everything on all levels, so we now make the definition of the tipping point of the physical world. It is the point at which the world of matter changes in obvious ways—you make a completely different choice and get a completely different result.

Part of this process is being willing to let go of how the change happens. When we completely release control on how something happens, and stay focused on the commitment to it happening, a whole other dimension of energy and force opens up for us, an opening that can, step by step, show us the path to the change we have chosen. You make the choice and the Creator makes the change. The difference between this phase and the others is similar to the difference between engagement and marriage.

> When you have touched death, you can see darkness...everywhere. Everything can become dark. You are in danger of reliving that darkness over and over. Forgiveness is the only way out. Sometimes forgiveness of others, but always forgiveness of yourself.
>
> The Raven

How I Met Tuhwuhch Tuhkraych (The Raven)

Ravens and crows have always been friends to me. At many intervals in my life, times of great transformation and profound change, they'd always be present and bring me comfort. It was when I moved to Los Angeles and experienced a series of deaths and losses that my relationship with them became telepathic. This was not a surprise, as their spiritual meaning is one of the void, a place in between, where time isn't linear, and unresolved past experiences live boldly with the present and create the future, a place where integrity, authenticity, and accountability are kings. A totem deserving of apparent awe, the raven represents the Creator himself.

As it had been with my father, two years prior to my mother's impending illness and death, Spirit began sending me definitive messages of the inevitable truth. It was my sister's fortieth birthday, and my mother and her husband had journeyed to Los Angeles for the celebration.

Mom and I had a nice, even relationship although she'd never travelled anywhere I lived just to visit me, like she had done for both of my sisters. I think, in theory, maybe it should have stung a little, but I think my understanding and early acceptance of my relationship with Mom enabled me not to focus on what we didn't have.

It wasn't but a few nights later, driving home from the birthday party, that I told Mom that earlier in the night, when she was chatting with her youngest brother Jim, Lee (her eldest brother who had crossed to the blue road several years before) had been standing in between them with his arms curved around both of their shoulders. As I told her, there Lee was again, smiling.

She said, "What?" as if she hadn't quite heard me.

I smiled and moved on with the conversation, knowing she'd heard me just fine.

Pleasantly toasty, at another of the many celebrations that week, I sat in the round booth next to Mom and somewhere between the second and fourth margarita she said, "You know you're going to have to take care of me," completely out of the blue.

Hmm, I thought. "What do you mean take care of you? Don't you want your favorite daughter to take care of you?"

It was a gentle ribbing I'd often have with her that we usually both giggled at. This time she looked at me straight on and said, "No, I am going to need *you* to take care of me."

Holy hell, I thought. I was drunk and she was serious. "Of course, Mom, I will take care of you," I said, taking her hand. Whew, thank God Faith interrupted the conversation just then, not knowing the gravity of it. My friend Faith; I thought that ironic.

A few months later as I was Christmas shopping at an estate sale, I found this wonderful 1920s print of a Dutch mother holding the hands of her young son and daughter. They were on the docks facing the ships coming in, and as the viewer of the portrait you saw their backs. It seemed so sweet and hopeful, I thought. *Mom will love this—I think this is her Christmas gift.*

Then the immediate response in my head was, *No, then you'd just have to take it back and it would be yours anyway.*

I wasn't quite sure where that came from, but I didn't want to let that portrait go, it so warmed my heart. I brought it home and promptly put it up on the wall of my bedroom. It was a few months down the road when Mom got her diagnosis of lung cancer. The time of reckoning was that first week home, immediately flying in after getting the news. I had gone quickly to the vitamin store to purchase some vitamin powder I really liked, hoping it would be helpful to her, but secretly trying to gain some control of—or at least to cope with—an out-of-control situation.

I made a glass for Mom and handed it to her, "No, I don't want this!" she exclaimed.

All of the messages and their meanings flooded in on her statement. I got it; in that moment, I got it. I wasn't taking care of her to help her live; I was taking care of her to help her die.

"Okay, Mom. I understand. I understand."

The raven had been a constant companion every day for those nine months, always showing up in an abounding way at the most devastating and crucial intervals of her illness. Having accepted my mother's choice from the beginning really helped me to receive comfort from all the sources through which it came, especially the raven.

Meeting the raven

My childhood home had been sold and I was saying the final good-bye. The day I made my final pilgrimage from Albuquerque, New Mexico, after selling the remainder of Mom's worldly possessions, I packed up the rented Explorer and was on my way back to Los Angeles. Generally, I'm not a fan of long road trips by myself, but for some reason I was excited about this one. I stopped for the night in Sedona, Arizona, and communed with the eagles in Boynton Canyon. It was late September so the days were still a little warm, the nights were crisp, clear, and laden with the soft scents of warm dirt and wild sage.

The next morning I was up and out by 11:00 so the Tuesday morning traffic on 89A was ghostly. As I made the right turn onto 89A and accelerated to about thirty miles an hour, I found my foot gently pressing on the brake until I had come to a complete stop. There was a huge raven in the middle of the road, and I mean huge; from my distance it looked to be almost four feet tall.

I was sitting there slightly awestruck. I'd never seen a raven that large. Then the raven became a man, who stood over six feet tall, dressed in buckskin pants, no shirt, but having massive wings and a headdress in the likeness of a raven's head with a lengthy beak that covered everything but the bottom of his face. In a split second he darted the hundred feet or so and rushed right through me, for a brief moment enveloping me completely. Just as quickly, he was gone.

I sat there amazed, overwhelmed, and out of breath with my hands clinched in the ten and two o'clock positions on the steering wheel. It felt as if I'd been having that experience for hours but in fact it was only a few seconds. After crying, sitting there in the middle of the road, I gathered together me and my wits and we headed back to Los Angeles.

THE DREAM STATE CAN BE AN EXCELLENT PLACE FOR A MEANINGFUL DIALOGUE WITH YOUR SPIRIT HELPER... BEGIN WITH YOUR FIRST PRAYERFUL ACTIVITY BY MAKING A POSITIVE AFFIRMATION THAT YOU WILL MEET YOUR ANIMAL TOTEM, YOUR SPIRIT HELPER, IN A MEANINGFUL DREAM THAT NIGHT WHEN YOU RETIRE.

BRAD STEIGER,
TOTEMS: THE TRANSFORMATIVE POWER OF YOUR ANIMAL TOTEMS

The Slayer's Ritual:

Mastering Your World through Awareness

Mastering your world by being in harmony with it is the goal. The only way to harmonize with something is to gain familiarity with it and this comes with practice. Everyone can run a sprint, but you are preparing for the marathon. Pay attention to the five elements below every day and keep a journal.

> *All of your experiences, and your awareness of them...lead you to this moment, until the next moment comes.*

What does this mean to you?

Every day your perspective shifts based on how you feel, what you are doing, and who you are around. Answer the question below, about the quote above, every day and see how the answers vary.

What is the cosmos doing?

We are mostly water, and our bodies are deeply affected by what the planets are doing. The more aware you become of your world, the more you'll want to expand your awareness of the moon cycles and Mercury retrograde, as well as solar and lunar eclipses. They all have a weighty impact during their cycles of influence.

Timing: Hour of power and biorhythms

Paying attention to the time of day you are naturally most alert, awake, comfortable, and present gives valuable information. Once you figure out what time that is, use it to begin a daily mindful meditation practice.

Paying attention to your environment: Synchronicity and messages from the creator

The Creator finds ways to communicate with you in whatever way you are open. All you have to do is listen. Look for your daily theme. Pay attention to words written on buses or advertisements, books or newspapers. Look for consistencies of your thoughts, feelings, and ideas; pay attention to what others are saying and doing around you. What is getting your attention and why is it valuable to you?

Animal totems: Symbolism

Many indigenous tribes believe that animals reveal themselves to us when they have a message to bring. Pay attention to any plant or animal totem that con-sistently gets your attention in any way. Animals can come to you in your dreams, in your television, in your thoughts, or in person. Any way they arrive is a message to you from the Creator. Maybe they have some advice on things you can strengthen or attri-butes you have in spades, but pay close attention, because they're talking to you

PART 4
Be Present

Demons can be very helpful, until they're not anymore

The Slayer's Weapons:

Stability, Trust, Leadership, Patience

The Story of Star Bear: Walking the Thin Line

He came into this world Poocheev Kweeyahguhtin in the year 1600, but people called him Star Bear. Born of a Weenuchiu Ute mother and a Cheyenne father, he was a blessing in spite of the circumstances—the Cheyenne and the Ute were known enemies.

His mother named him Star Bear because she believed he came from the stars; she considered the cosmos his father as the real story was too much to bear. Being born at the turn of a century was a harbinger of Star Bear's great power. The best tracker in all the west, north, and south, Star Bear was a genius of his day. He truly was like no other, and it was that uniqueness that made him invaluable to all the tribes and even their enemies. Star Bear had what we call now a photographic memory, but at the time he was a real black swan.

He also possessed other gifts—wisdom, vision, and foresight—which on many levels brought him a subtle loneliness. There were no stories of his father on anyone's lips. Everyone knew what had happened but it was considered disrespectful to his mother to speak of it and Star Bear didn't want that. Instead Star Bear longed for the father he conjured in his mind. He knew that if he just did his work, that someday he would meet his father.

Star Bear led many but really followed none, except for *Sinawaf*, the One above. The days were long in the high desert, and there was always much to do, especially during harvest. Star Bear spent his time teaching his people about the plants and medicinal herbs of the area and about the most efficient way to track for food and other needs. Relationships between the other tribes and the colonial and Spanish settlers were fragile. No one had experienced the level of ignorance and selfishness that came with the settlers. Among many things, the settlers were survivors, and people trying to survive could be vicious. Star Bear had created a reputation in the area for his ability to mediate any situation. This made him a commodity for his people, selling his services to friends and enemies and somehow being respected by everyone.

The people of the Pueblos and the Plains knew that times were changing irrevocably; keeping things moving and peaceful as long as possible was truly the best they could hope for. They all knew that each person must do his or her part. Star Bear became indispensable both to the settlers and to his people, who he kept out from under colonial control.

The years turned one into another and another, and Star Bear's longing never really seemed to show on his face, although it was always there just to the side of all the other things—until the day everything changed. Star Bear was taking a group of French tradesmen down into Northern New Mexico to a mission, in order to procure a new labor force where the slave trade was in full effect. It was rumored that their original group of enslaved Cherokee had all died of dysentery. It was beginning to be widely known that the native tribes didn't do well with European diseases and many were dying. They had a new group of Cheyenne that they hoped would last a little longer.

There seemed to be a mist caught in the canyon as they rode into the mission area. The dawn was just breaking. It was cold that morning but the snow seemed to be disappearing as quickly as it came. Star Bear looked around the encampment but didn't see anyone. Then he heard the painful shrill of a woman's cry. He looked over to a makeshift enclosure where they kept the enslaved ones. It barely offered any protection from the elements let alone the bitter cold. He saw a woman on her knees wailing in grief, with a young boy standing next to her. Star Bear's heart moved and his eyes moistened. Two men were carrying the lifeless body of a man. Star Bear knew he was dead, because even from that long distance he could see the blue around his lips. He'd seen that death on many. Star Bear stood mesmerized for a moment. He knew they were the ones he was waiting for.

> He knew that if he just did his work, that someday he would meet his father and know. Star Bear led many, but really followed none, except for Sinawaf, the One Above.

Star Bear exhaled, and then—as if lightning struck near his feet—moved quickly and with the force and timing of a condor swooped down, scooping the woman by her waist and grabbing the young boy's arm, moving them swiftly behind the enclosure. While the woman and her son appeared to be startled, they offered no resistance and didn't really seem surprised. Star Bear, as gently as he could, threw them one after another onto the travois and sharply covered them with a couple of hides.

There were six in his group including Star Bear, and this was his last stop. The Frenchmen had taken their things and would be joining another tracker for the journey to New Orleans. Star Bear picked up a few supplies and made his political rounds. Although he never shook hands with anyone, he had their trust and an ear when needed. He made it clear to anyone watching that he really needed to start his way back as the sun was fully over the horizon now. He placed the supplies on the travois, hoisted himself onto the back of his horse, and rode away with his two unwitting passengers and no one was the wiser.

Star Bear knew they needed medicine even though they didn't seem to be showing any symptoms. He would take another route back where the herbs needed for the medicine usually grew in abundance, at least in the high season. Time was of the essence. They needed to get to the river before dusk. There wasn't enough food for the three of them and there would be plenty to do before the stars and moon took over.

It had been at least an hour now. Star Bear made sure that no one was around and that they hadn't been followed. It was now safe to stop. Uncovering them, they all took a long look at one another. He spoke to them in Cheyenne, although it seemed that no words were necessary. Her name was Asha (hope) and her son was Hiamovi (whirlwind), and now he understood. Again his heart moved and his eyes moistened; so much is carried in a name. He gave them what little food he had left from the previous day, some water, and packed them up again for the remainder of the day's ride. The midday sun would soon be high in the sky.

Finally reaching the place where the river runs through the canyon, he could see the fish biting at the top of the water, a unique phenomenon at this time of year. Just before dusk was the most efficient time to fish. Star Bear hoped that Asha and Hiamovi were feeling strong enough to help as the sun was on his descent, and the fish weren't going to catch themselves. Upon arrival, Asha immediately set off to find a suitable sleeping place with firewood for the fire, and Hiamovi took Star Bear's knife and whittled the end of a long stick to a sharp point for fishing, like his father had taught him.

Star Bear hadn't said anything, but was quietly relieved. The evening seemed to be peaceful yet vibrant; the air was crisp and dry, and all the animals were out eating and drinking during the golden hour. This one was particularly rich with change. He was stirring the medicine over the fire when Hiamovi ran up to him laying out the four fish he'd caught. Star Bear nodded his approval, and again his heart moved and his eyes moistened; Hiamovi smiled ear to ear and ran off to help his mother.

Taking a deep breath, Star Bear walked to the river's edge and when he knelt to splash some cold water on his face he felt the full weight of his emotion piercing through his back and crashing through his heart. After Star Bar heaved over and let out a dense cry, the tears came with a fury. As he grappled to catch his breath and the tears cleared from his eyes, he found his face just inches from the water. He then saw the reflection; it was a face similar to his but not his own. He stared at it in confusion for a few moments. He could see the image of the largest bear he'd ever seen shimmering in the water around his shadow, and he felt no fear. Then he felt the presence of the bear. This was the spirit that had guided him all his life, the comfort more familiar than any family member.

The bear spoke: "My son, the time has come for you to know the truth about your birth. It was the fifth full moon of the year, and your father, born of Cheyenne blood, was raiding your mother's village. It was just meant to be for food and supplies, but your father saw your mother and her fear enraged him. Your father was angry about many things and often expressed it to his own ends. He saw her fear as weakness and he beat and raped her right there where she stood. You were born seven moons later and considered a miracle by the entire tribe. Your mother asked that no one speak of the night you were conceived ever, even if you asked. She didn't want you to be haunted by your father's spirit or your mother's pain."

Star Bear wept as he listened; somehow he had always known.

The bear continued, "You have walked the very thin line of righteousness that has been laid out for you, never wavering, always preserving the greater good with your choices even when it appeared that neither choice was good. Star Bear, every man will follow his truth until he finds the truth, and you have followed this path with immense vigor, discipline, and faith. Therefore you have created no more ripples in the great water. Asha and Hiamovi are your reward, and in time they will be your family."

"Thank you, Sinawaf," Star Bear uttered. "And do not worry for your mother—she is at peace now and gives her blessing on your family. Now go, the night is not over yet."

And with that the bear disappeared.

Star Bear walked back to camp feeling as if he'd been gone for hours. Asha was just beginning to clean the fish. Dinner that night was the best that anyone'd ever had, for different reasons of course. Asha was safe. Hiamovi was full. Star Bear had found what he was searching for, and they all took the medicine and went to sleep.

> You have walked the very thin line of righteousness that has been laid out for you, never wavering, always preserving the greater good with your choices even when it appeared that neither choice was good.
>
> The bear

Pride and the Devil

Demons are known for making promises—of power, control, protection, information, and even help. Often it is our human self-pride that desires all of those things in order to protect ourselves. Pride is our first protector, the first line of defense that we have. But it is our dignity that will deliver us from all things. Sometimes demons do help, until the person asking for the help has grown beyond their ability to help.

I've worked with many people who, as children, were abused or afflicted in some way, who in their time of desperation and need asked for help and were answered by a not-so-well-meaning critter. For some time they lived with their new friends and were given strength, knowledge, and protection, or they were led right into more pain and chaos. As they grew up their friendly critter became more of a burden than a help, and the battle with it became formidable.

I was about eight years old when my best friend, Jenna, and I were walking to the Circle K, on a beautiful, clear summer morning. We had just been at the local public pool, a place we had spent every summer day since we were three, and were wearing our swimsuits. It was a quick, straight shot across the park. As we had just entered the Circle K parking lot, a man in a convertible pulled up and asked us if we knew where the pool was; he said he was going there.

I pointed to the pool, which was visible from where we were standing, and said, "It's right there."

He replied, "I don't want to get lost. Can you get in and show me?"

"*No!*" I said.

But then my friend walked up to the car door, looked at me, and said, "It will be okay."

And as I was yelling at her not to get into the car, she was in and they were pulling away. When he made a right turn going in the opposite direction from the pool, I knew my fears for her would be realized. I was devastated and not sure what to do. I ran across the park to her house and told her mother what happened. We called the police and waited. About four hours later, I was standing on the sidewalk in front of her house, when I saw her walking up the street, crying. The man had dropped her off after molesting her, and she'd walked the rest of the way home.

Her story and struggle are devastating and ongoing, as one might expect, and it is my hope that through the exploration of my story and the revelations that have come to me over a lifetime that some sort of restoration can occur for us and anyone else that suffers in this way.

It took me years of working in the healing industry to finally look towards the very event that had inspired my need to understand demons, the Devil, and my belief in complete healing for those who are afflicted. I carried such guilt about my friend's experience. I went over and over the events of that morning, thinking about what I could have done to prevent it. I should have grabbed her arm and not allowed her to get in the car. I should have screamed louder rather than just be a voice of reason. Certainly, I could have done something. She and I have been indelibly linked ever since, and although we were never as close as we were in childhood, there have been times over the years when we have reconnected. I have kept track of, and been witness to, many of her sufferings.

> For some time they lived with their new friends and were given strength, knowledge, and protection—or they were led right into more pain and chaos. As they grew up their friendly critter became more of a burden than a help, and the battle with it became formidable.

Some knowledge of her sufferings I have received in visions and dreams, and some I've received firsthand. It wasn't until about five years ago when I reconnected with Jenna's family that I was able to talk about our shared experiences. It was from that moment onward that things began to change for me regarding this memory. Finally, the enormous weight I carried, the frustration and sadness I felt, began to give way to what I really saw and experienced on that day and many days since.

During a long conversation we had, her sister assured me that what happened to Jenna wasn't my fault. No one had ever said that out loud...especially me. In fact, I never really spoke about it at any length with anyone—ever. When she said those words it occurred to me that I'd burdened myself with a deep sense of responsibility for not having stopped the event from happening. After all, every time I thought about it I'd come to the same conclusion: there truly was nothing I could have done. I had such intense guilt, and I couldn't rationally reconcile what for. A couple of weeks after that conversation I had a dreamtime vision. Specifically, I traveled back in time, as the person I am today, to heal Jenna's childhood home, a place where I'd spent countless joyous hours with her family. And to see and feel consciously what I had missed before.

The home was a brown, square, adobe-looking, flat-roofed stucco home that is traditional for the Southwest. I breached the front door with a vengeance. To be in that house as an adult was strange; the entire place was so small, where it once seemed so roomy. I felt like the FBI on a drug raid. The ceilings were lower than I remembered, and the energy was cold.

As a child, I loved spending time with my friend and her family; they seemed so happy and content together in that place. Feeling the chill of fear and despair, I was certain that their happiness must've been quite a feat to accomplish with the nature of the energy in the house. I found myself beating on the walls, calling out the demons and any other entities that were present. All the doors and windows were open, and a strong wind began to blow through. All the dark spirits that had inhabited the home and the land began to flow out. Archangel Michael and his angels were outside waiting to deliver or transform them into usable energy for the planet. I could tell by my ferocity the dense nature and strength of the entities leaving. Soon, all the darkness was gone and there was only sunlight, but I still wasn't settled. I hadn't yet found what I was looking for. As I walked out of the house, I woke up.

I sat up in bed and took a deep breath. As a child I felt everything, but clearly had no words for what I felt and saw, and no one to share it with. Somehow, connecting with a witness to my childhood had shown me some of the things I had perceived but had no words for. Finally, I had taken a trip home and was anxiously awaiting a long-overdue meeting with Jenna's mother. I always had such a deep love for her as if she were my own mother; we shared a special spiritual kinship that was always soothing to me.

After all the years she said to me, "Tracee, I am so sorry you had to go through this as well. I understand now that we were all so focused on Jenna that we completely overlooked how horrifying this must have been for you. I can still see you standing on the driveway, alone and afraid, waiting for her to come home. I didn't even take the time to hold and comfort you. I am really sorry."

The grown-up in me appreciated those words, as no one—including my family—had ever thought to acknowledge me. The child in me wept and for the first time felt safe. I'd had many run-ins with the destruction created by evil, but I'd never experienced any human understanding of my experiences. The adults in my life weren't able to protect me or give me any understanding at the time. Our meeting was profoundly touching for me because she was able to say things to me on my mother's behalf, things my mom wasn't able to say.

It wasn't more than a week after our conversation that I was home washing the dishes when my mind flashed back to the very moment that Jenna got in the car and I saw it. It was a demon, a little wiry critter with what looked like several small horns on the top of its head and red eyes. It had its hands on her shoulders, guiding her into the vehicle. After she'd opened the door, she looked at me, and I will never forget that look in her eyes because it was in that moment that the demon looked at me and said, "Ha! She's mine now."

I lost my breath and held onto the sink while the tears came. That was the information that was missing all this time and the key to my guilt. My feelings of guilt had been pointing me to what I really saw that day, with whom the real battle was, and for whom I was looking in her house that day I went back in my vision. Every day, I continue to pray for my friend and her battle for her soul, and when I get the call, I will be ready. I was finally free.

> If we feel positive, we feel good; and when we feel negative, we feel guilty. Truly, no matter where we are on the continuum of positive to negative, they are two equal ends of the same message from the Creator...or from the reflection of our self.

The Slayer's Path: Always Be Present

The Devil only has power in other dimensions: the past and the future. Staying in the present moment during times of great distress can give you the power that you need to do what you can. Make no mistake: eventually you will address the past, and there is a way to do it with presence and strength. You can pass through the underworld with faith, knowledge, and protection using the strength of your present moment.

The angle of light

I sat around one morning on the porch pondering stuff. It was a beautiful spring day, bright and clear. As I looked towards my left I noticed a single strand of spider silk that was illuminated by the sun. When I adjusted my vision just a little further to the left, it seemed to disappear. Obviously it did not. I just couldn't see it.

I sat up in my chair and said, "Thank you Creator. Yes, it is all about the angle of light."

In our culture we are nurtured to focus on the amount of light and not on the angle. We focus on if we feel positive or negative, and we judge ourselves to whatever varying degree we experience negativity and positivity. If we feel positive, we feel good; and when we feel negative, we feel guilty. Truly, no matter where we are on the continuum of positive to negative, they are two equal ends of the same message from the Creator... or from the reflection of our self. It is when we allow ourselves to begin to open up to the angle of light that we can accurately interpret the information that we receive.

The Slayer's Path: **Always Be Present**

How to stay in the moment

Honesty and acceptance are the two golden rules of staying present. Honesty means being honest with yourself about who you are, how you feel, and what you think is paramount in knowing how to proceed in any direction. The Devil's goal is to influence you to remain stagnant and lie to yourself as much as possible. The Devil works by influencing you to put your focus on the shame and guilt of what has happened or the fear regarding what may happen in the future. Having fear, shame, humiliation, or guilt is a very powerful message from the Creator. I call them the four arrows.

The four arrows

I call fear, shame, humiliation, and guilt *arrows* because they are energy you generate that focuses in on yourself. Each energy arrow focuses your attention to a different place: fear is an arrow to your vision, shame an arrow to your voice, humiliation an arrow to your power, and guilt an arrow to your heart. When you are hit by any one of these arrows, you must ask yourself the following questions: What am I not seeing? What am I not saying? Where do I feel powerless? What am I not allowing myself to feel?

It is a natural instinct when we experience these deep and invasive emotions to feel at fault in some way—and it's true that we are at fault. We are generating these emotions as a message to our conscious mind that we have needs that aren't being met. If we can understand that we have created the emotion to point out where we have power and choice in the situation, then we can effect a change. Answering each question will guide you to where movement and change can take place, and where there is movement, there is change. In accepting any of these feelings, you embrace the new knowledge that your acceptance and, inevitably, understanding of these emotions will bring.

Be here now

Staying in the moment means that you commit yourself fully to whatever you are doing. It is our human nature to be multidimensional. However, it takes education and development to maintain and balance your awareness on all the necessary elements of action. When driving a car, you have to take into account various factors, like the car itself, the road, and other cars—just for starters. Other influences could include weather, dysfunction in the car or road, or a change in perception for any reason.

Learning to contend with all of these variables takes practice. At the beginning driving a car, for me, was a bit tumultuous. I totaled three vehicles by the time I was seventeen. Luckily, I was mostly prone to hitting stationary things like parked cars or poles. The same dynamic happens as you begin to open up your psychic channels to hear, see, and feel other dimensions of energy while still being present to your physical reality. It is commonly believed that women and adolescents are most prone to psychic phenomena; and in previous eras that has been the case.

Psychic awareness is related to the movement of *kundalini energy* in the physical body. As this energy activates different glands in the body, a different level of energy and awareness is opened to the individual. Today, because of the extraordinary energy shift on the planet, everyone—not just women and adolescents—is experiencing intense shifts in consciousness in ways that may be abrupt and new to them. Staying in the moment means always being able to bring whatever you are focusing on into the physical moment.

STANDING IN THE PRESENCE OF THE UNKNOWN ALL HAVE THE SAME RIGHT TO THINK, AND ALL ARE EQUALLY INTERESTED IN THE GREAT QUESTIONS OF ORIGIN AND DESTINY.

ROBERT INGERSOLL

Ask a question and answer it

One of the most common things that folks do in times of confusion is ask questions. Why is this happening? Where did that come from? How did I get here? When a question is asked, a new dimension of energy is opened, based on the intent of the question. For example, "Why is this happening to me?" When the question is generated on any level it sends out a stream of energy that begins to attract the answer. If you are going to ask the question, you've got to be open to the answer. Interestingly, it is just as common to remain focused on the question and never receive the answer. Unfortunately, if the question goes unanswered it generates energy in another dimension that can leave you spiritually anchored to the question.

Savannah in the summer

Every time I travel, I do healings for the city and the location where I stay. One incredibly hot and humid summer, I traveled to Savannah, Georgia. Luckily, the mosquitos were fairly tame that year, but the heat was strong and had awakened me early one morning around five. I was staying at a little bed-and-breakfast that was originally an old colonial single-family home built in 1857. I made a cup of coffee and came out to the front stoop where there was just room enough for a bench before you started down the first steps to the street.

I sat there as the sun was rising and started my prayer. I asked for the assistance of the Creator and called in Jesus and St. Michael, and then I called to any spirits who'd been left behind or needed help to transition. Normally, in places that hold such layered spiritual history, I expect at least some of the people coming forward to be connected to history that is familiar to me, but this time out was different. Only about five became present.

The one story that is still clear as if it were yesterday is of a little boy held in limbo. He came to me asking, "Why?" He was about ten years old, wearing tan-colored overalls and a light-colored shirt. His blonde hair was a tussle, and his pale skin was flush and sweaty. I saw that his home, a farmhouse, had been burnt to the ground, and with it went his entire family. Everyone had transitioned easily except for him. He was in shock and distraught as he kept asking "Why?"

I traveled deeper into his paradigm, looking for the answer he was seeking, and a voice came

"No answer that was given was sufficient to comfort his sorrow and loss. He must accept his fate and join his family, and then his questions can be answered."

I gasped in a deep breath as the tears started to flow. I explained that for him right now, nothing he could hear would make his fate feel acceptable, yet he must accept it. I told him how sorry I was for his experience and told him his family was waiting for his arrival. They loved and missed him so much.

Just as I was saying that to him, the distress left his face. He could see and feel his family and the angels with them. He was no longer distraught and afraid. He looked at me gently, and then he was gone.

I sat for a few more moments and felt the warmth of the sun drying the tears on my face. The din of the morning traffic had begun and my job was complete.

> It is when we allow ourselves to begin to open up to the angle of light that we can accurately interpret the information that we receive.

The Slayer's Motto: Do Nothing until You Know What to Do

To a slayer, the ability to discern when to act is her most prized possession. In the spiritual world, everything is eternal and ongoing. The spiritual world is the place, ultimately, where change must be made for healing to occur. Having said that, the Devil wants you to act rashly and take as little time as possible to make decisions, knowing that you'll likely make mistakes acting out of your emotional responses or without thinking.

If there is one thing that I've learned, it's that there is always time, no matter the situation. All things will inevitably be reconciled. However, it may take lifetimes, so it's best to do nothing until you know exactly what to do. Learning to trust your intuition and instinct is the most valuable tool that you have. Your intuition and instinct allow you to be prepared and ready to act with precision.

> Mama and Papa Bear have much to teach about leadership and its true meaning, self-reflection and self-love, joy in resurrecting a pure heart, and physical strategies to sustain a healthful and balanced way of life.

My bear ally

Two times in my life, during profound times of transformation, the bear has come to me in a dream. The first time was when I began working as a spiritual empath. The first three years were the most intense; I barely slept and rarely went outside. My inner world was rich with new knowledge and experience, but my body was wrought with fatigue. I don't suppose it helped that I was on the Carl's Jr. diet. You see, since about the age of twelve, I had always been weight- and health-conscious, but after contracting an illness that required the adoption of extreme measures, I stopped eating sugar, drinking alcohol, and became vegan. I learned about supplements and herbs, and with these choices came a complete physical recovery and the beginning of an opportunity to heal myself emotionally and then spiritually.

The Slayer's Motto:
Do Nothing until You Know What to Do

The spiritual healing was a lengthy process that took several years of daily work. All of it was awe-inspiring. At about the time I began working with clients, I had been quite healthful for about a decade, so I allowed myself to enjoy soda, burgers, and fries on occasion. My indulgence was only about once a month for about two years and the freedom alone to eat what I wanted when I wanted was invaluable. But the physical fatigue from the spiritual and emotional transformation was mounting. One evening, after several nights of very little sleep and extreme emotions, I prayed to the Creator for some relief and a new strategy. That night I fell fast asleep and woke up in the middle of a dream sleeping in the warm clutches of big Mama Bear.

For the first time in months, I felt calm and at peace. Safety was truly not a feeling I'd been accustomed to until that moment, and it was overwhelming. I wept to create space to receive this feeling of safety and comfort for the first time in my life. That night the bear told me what was next. It was now time to eat only the things that brought nourishment to my body. Taking a leadership position in my life meant that it was time to walk through my fear of sharing who I really was and not hiding any of my abilities. Finally, that compassion meant setting boundaries with people instead of just understanding that they do not know the impact that they have on me and others.

The freedom in opinion

The second time the bear joined me in dreamtime was just recently. This time it was Papa Bear. He brought me the message of safety, comfort, and compassion as before, but this time the message was distinctly different. As we sat face to face, his message was to have enormous courage and strength with a physical vitality I hadn't experienced since I was a child. He told me that my opinion had value. This struck me as funny, because anyone who knows me knows that I am not necessarily shy about my opinion.

It then became clear to me that my emphasis has always been on understanding and having compassion. And while having empathy for both sides of any situation is definitely a skill set, it was now time truly to cultivate my own opinion. A freedom opened in my heart that day, a new level of trust—in the Creator, in myself, and in others—that took me deeply into the consciousness of safety.

You've got a friend in bear

So, should you seek the assistance of the bear, you will indeed have a powerful ally. The bear brings a new comfort in the truth and an integration of understanding. Mama and Papa Bear have much to teach about leadership and its true meaning, self-reflection and self-love, joy in resurrecting a pure heart, and physical strategies to sustain a healthful and balanced way of life.

The Slayer's Pact: Don't Give Up

The only possible way that you can lose a battle with a demon is to give up…and even then, you have an eternity to be inspired into a new strategy, so your victory is inevitably assured. It's true that as people get smarter and stronger, sometimes their demons do too. Ultimately, when you are ready, willing, and able to face your deepest fears, that's when you garner the support and resources you need to overcome the battles and win the war for your soul.

There is an uncanny phenomenon that I've encountered when working with afflicted people and their demons. A demon always makes itself known, even when its goal is to deceive or mislead you into believing that it isn't there. Demons have some telltale signs of their presence and although there are many presentations, they have some commonalities that most people experience.

The Slayer's Pact: **Don't Give Up**

Important signs of demonic presence

Demons are present when someone who isn't usually biblical, starts getting biblical, using words like *evil, blasphemous, sin,* and *sinner* or other biblical references, or in some way starts to imbibe that ancient, biblical world view.

Demons are also incredibly vulgar and are usually pretty keen on knowing what vulgarities to use to create the most fear or disgust in those they torment. They'll call you a whore and a thief and use every curse word in the dictionary, saying whatever they need to in their assault on your esteem: *fat, ugly, broken, unwanted, unlovable*…whatever you need to hear to be worn down into feeling powerless and hopeless.

They'll talk about killing, death, dying, and the possibility of hurting your loved ones, if they are threatened.

They will laugh in your face and tell you no one cares and no one can help you.

Most of all, they want you to believe that they will never leave you alone.

Remember that the things they say are personally designed for you and your beliefs and triggers. Facing your own fears will leave nothing for the demon to be attached to.

The fiery dimension of hell

I used to think that a lost soul was a profound tragedy, until I came to understand that healing was inevitable, that those who were lost would eventually be found, that those who suffered loss would be reconciled, and that those who hurt others would eventually understand the pain they created. This was the meaning of karma. Having said that, hell exists with fire and all—scaly demons with horns and red eyes, sometimes claws and tails.

The experience of hell is a particular dimension of energy that those who experience it have become open to. This dimensional awareness can be passed down to descendants. It can be transferred through a violent act or sexual encounter or triggered by the use of drugs and self-violence. This demonic dimension is not common to everyone, but for those who perceive it, it is terrifying and tumultuous.

> Remember that the things they say are personally designed for you and your beliefs and triggers. Facing your own fears will leave nothing for the demon to be attached to.

These demons appear scary and relentless. Their only power, however, comes from convincing you to believe that you are eternally afflicted with them. Again, facing your fears, being honest and open about your deepest and darkest secrets, and going back in time and space to the origin of the event that opened you to their existence are ways to stop the affliction.

If this is your path, profound and brutal honesty with yourself is your savior.

Past and present dimensions

Energetically speaking, the only way that the past is left in the past is when it is completely neutral and reconciled in the present time. Your spirit keeps a record of every experience and feeling that you have. When you have traumatic feelings and experiences that haven't been fully worked through on all of the other levels of perception, the experience is very much in your present world even if you ignore it, set it aside, and cover it with compensating behaviors. This unreconciled energy can also be passed down to future generations, it can be transferred to another person who is better suited to process it, or it can be carried with your soul into subsequent incarnations.

Three times the charm?

I'd been in New York City for maybe a year, when I met a woman at an art gallery opening. And, within five minutes of conversation, this woman told me she had been raped by the same man three times. He was a man she didn't know; he knew her schedule and three times he had waited for her outside her apartment building in the middle of the night and raped her when she got home from work.

I was stunned on many levels. Everything about the conversation seemed ridiculous, but I also felt deeply that she was telling the truth. Of course, I asked what the police said, and she confided that she'd not called them. The rapist said he'd hurt her family, and she was terrified. My mind was full of questions that she could not, in her current state of terror, answer for me.

I wasn't surprised in the least that she was telling me all of this. I listened intently, and when there was no more for her to say I contemplated for a minute before speaking. "You have more courage and power than you know. When you are ready, you will stop this man."

She sighed a little in relief, as did I. The host of the party interrupted our conversation, she excused herself, and I didn't see her again.

Whew, I thought—*karma.*

It is easy to sit outside a situation involving another person and judge them for what you think they should do, or even sometimes, what you think you would do in the same situation, but there were way too many unanswered questions. Who was this woman? Who was this man? What was their connection and history? Why did she do nothing? What was the power he had over her? What was it that she needed in order to stop the situation from continuing? Would an outside source stop the situation? Would it ever be stopped?

Understand that all of these questions must now be answered; they are dimensions of energy that have been opened. When this lady came to me, she came to share her burden, she opened a door to me that I accepted by listening and energetically and emotionally researching answers for her. I closed the door when I gave her my answer (or in this case, my thoughts), and now I'll close the door on all of these questions as well.

What, were you born in a barn?

Who was this woman? *A slayer.*

Who was this man? *A terrorist.*

What was their connection and history? *I don't care.*

Why did she do nothing? *Because her obligation was bigger than her fear of him and his assaults.*

What was the power he had over her? *For me, it didn't matter.*

What was it that she needed in order to stop the situation from continuing? *To wake up out of her past vulnerability into her current strength.*

Would an outside source stop the situation? *No.*

Would it ever be stopped? *Yes.*

When you open a door, you must close it when you are through. My mother would always say, "What, were you born in a barn?" You can only know someone's suffering by putting yourself in their position, which means their ways, their beliefs, and their relationships to their experiences. Empathy is the way we do this, and when we have the ability to empathize with someone, it is because we resonate with them in some way. Maybe we have similar experiences, beliefs, or feelings on a level we are aware, or on a level we are not.

Empathy means freedom

Now I really want you to pay attention here. If you get nothing else from this book, get this. Crying and the truthful expression of emotion—grieving—is the one thing that transforms our old, dense energy and invites new light into our energy system and into our body. It is the presence of this new light and information that helps us achieve understanding. Folks really take a hit when it comes to this because in households around the world crying and the expression of emotion are perceived as weaknesses or as demonstrations of a lack of self-mastery. It is not the lack of crying that is the mastery—it is the acceptance of its necessity and the submission to it, with mastery. That is the goal.

The aura

Your physical body has an energy system called an aura. It is composed of different vibrational layers of energy, through which we express and interpret our thoughts and emotions, among other things. Your aura is the way that your body conducts energy through its energy centers called *chakras*, which are vortices just in front and in back of the physical body. A chakra brings in new energy, and—sort of like an exhaust system—it releases energy that no longer serves you.

Your chakras also give out your light to others. How much a slayer energetically gives or takes, to or from his environment, depends upon how spiritually developed he is. Those in struggle will, for a time, take more from others than they are able to give.

> Understanding the energy system helps you understand how your mind, body, and spirit process information. As you begin to understand just how easy it is to break things down into little bite-sized pieces, it will make everything in your life more digestible, manageable, and joyful.

The aura is connected to the physical body through the central nervous system and through your roadmap of glands we call the endocrine system, which serves as a direct pipeline to your brain and neural networks. *Kundalini* is the life-force evolutionary energy, or sexual energy (and by *sexual*, we mean it seeks to connect or unify the body, mind, and spirit).

Kundalini energy (called *chi* in Chinese) is generated from the body at the base of the spine and travels up the spine to the brain and back down again. As it travels up and down the spine, the kundalini passes through the various chakras at certain developmental stages in your life. As you develop spiritually, the kundalini energy activates your endocrine glands. For example, the kundalini activates the pituitary gland at the beginning of puberty.

Throughout history, there is evidence of the recognition of this energy system in almost every culture, including Cherokee, Mayan, Tibetan, ancient Jewish, Hindu, and Egyptian. The most widely known formulation of the energy system is Hindu. While there are literally hundreds of energy vortices in the many layers of energy bodies that make up who we are, I have put together a simplified combination of the chakra and energy system that I have found to best describe the information I needed while going through the spiritual process. I do encourage you to do your own research on this subject because it is vast and fascinating.

Your aura has four basic layers and ten chakras to be discussed here: the etheric layer or body double (habits), the emotional body (also called astral body), the mental body (thoughts), and the causal body (higher vibrational spirit). Each energy center will receive and transmit energy from the layers of the aura that will be translated by your thoughts and feelings for transmutation (processing) through the central nervous system and endocrine system in the physical body. The auric fields will receive information and translate it to the mind, emotions, and physical body. It is through the healing of the auric fields of energy that the physical body may also heal.

The auric field processes in this way. Have you ever been talking about or writing something and you cannot think of the word you need? Well, this happens to me all of the time. So, when I can't think of the word I want, I call my sister. She's as sharp as a tack, and just the act of connecting with her helps me connect to the word I want, even if we don't speak. My mental body can connect to hers and I'll fall into alignment with her focus. Just as I help others tune in with their emotional bodies as an empath, she likewise helps me focus.

There are many more chakras, sub-chakras, and layers to the energy system. Here I align the basic chakras to the energy bodies to help you make the connection to their interaction. Although this information may not be new for some of you, make sure to scan it anyway, just to make sure that you have the understanding and ability to apply it for use here. Understanding the energy system helps you understand how your mind, body, and spirit process information. As you begin to understand just how easy it is to break things down into little bite-sized pieces, it will make everything in your life more digestible, manageable, and joyful—especially in times where it doesn't appear to be any of these things.

The etheric body

The etheric body is the layer of energy next to your skin. It is often referred to as the *body double*. Your physical body mimics the energy pattern of the body double, which is itself created by the information in all of the other layers of energy. Our daily habits and responses to things reside here. You will find it referred to as the *lowest common denominator* in other chapters in the book.

The etheric body is connected to the root chakra and governs the fulfillment of your basic needs for food, shelter, and self-preservation. It also keeps you anchored in your physical body and connected to Mother Earth. Someone whose attention is centered here may express more of these particular emotions: fear, paranoia, anger, distrust, and loss or fear of loss. Their belief systems will also be rooted in self-preservation. This chakra is related to your fight-or-flight mechanism in the physical body created by the pancreas and islets of Langerhans (two little but powerful glands found in the pancreas). When these glands are alerted, they create chemicals that stimulate acute awareness and strength when danger is perceived.

Root chakra (first chakra): Processes the fulfillment of basic needs and your connection to the planet; governs the legs and thighs and base of spine. Color: red.

Foot chakras (tenth chakra): The feet are your connectors to the earth and what grounds you and solidifies your direction. They can access and release your deepest fear and access and embrace the all-encompassing love and energetic nourishment from the planet. Through the feet you discover new paths. Color: Coral

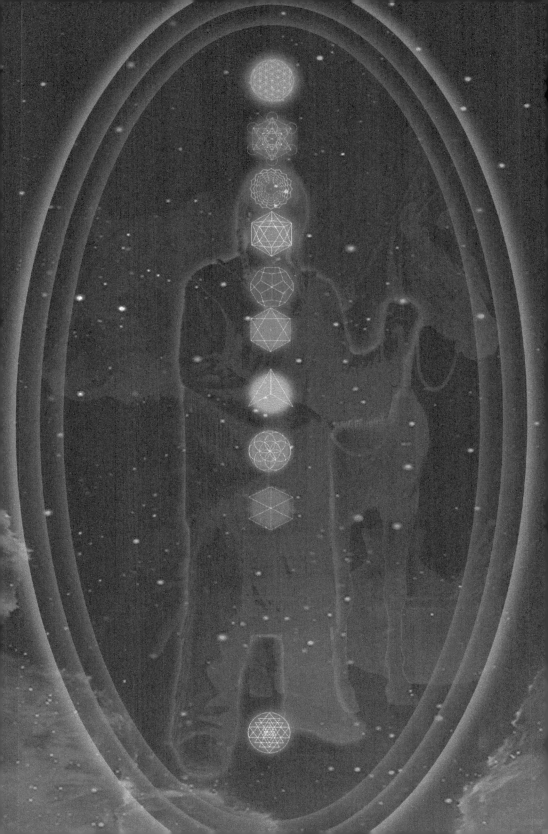

The emotional body

After the etheric body, the emotional body is the next layer out. The emotional body is connected to the navel/spleen chakra, the solar plexus chakra, the heart chakra, and the medulla chakra. It keeps a digital imprint of all of your currently running emotional patterns, in addition to old, unresolved patterns and grief. It holds your emotional reactions and responses that on some level you feel vital to your survival. It is the layer that contains your memories of trauma and of loss, as well as of success and joy. The emotional body also alerts your instinct, heart, and mind to your surroundings, and can often trigger the fight-or-flight instinct if conflict is perceived.

Conflict on this level can take the form of anything from physical danger to mental and emotional danger. A sense of mental and emotional danger might arise, for instance, when you notice that you are crossing paths with someone who does not hold the same beliefs as you.

This chakra also governs sexual energy and desire, but because it is connected to raw emotion, it is easy to misperceive someone who is emotionally raw or sensitive as being highly sexual. The confusion of sexual discovery early in a relationship is often the result of this type of miscalculation: You might think someone likes you or is attracted to you because they are emotionally open or raw. When the emotional body is overwhelmed, depression can result. The emotions that are often expressed through these chakras are love, desire, joy, fear, anxiety, confusion, creativity, guilt, obsession, and compassion.

In the physical body, your emotions will be expressed through your sexual organs, pancreas, liver, kidneys, gallbladder, heart, lungs, stomach, spleen, and entire intestinal and bowel tract. This body also governs your natural body weight balance. The emotional body is connected to the pituitary, thyroid, hypothalamus, and thymus glands. People who fluctuate in their body weight often have ungrieved emotional pain, trauma, past-life experiences, and a hypersensitivity to multidimensional energy, a hyperawareness that makes one empathetic or psychic.

Navel/spleen chakra (second chakra): Processes emotions, and governs the spleen and reproductive organs, as well as the glandular system and kundalini energy. Color: orange.

Solar plexus chakra (third chakra): Processes your relationship to the outside world and your self-esteem; governs your digestive tract. Color: yellow.

Heart chakra (fourth chakra): Processes the energy of love and compassion and governs the heart and lungs. Color: green.

Time chakra (eighth): The medulla/ time chakra lies at the base of the skull and holds all of your Akashic records (the energy, information, and memories of your past that are vital to your current evolutionary cycle). Working with this chakra will teach you how to stay in the present moment by working through the energies that reside there. Color: light violet blue.

The mental body

The mental body is the next layer out from the emotional body and contains a recording of your beliefs about yourself, others, and the world. It connects you to your ability to process information through thought and analysis, through your rational thinking. Such thinking is often linear in scope and helps the brain to process the concept of life as past, present, or future.

The mental body uses dynamics, like strategy and tactics, to navigate life experiences. The mental body is also connected to your ability to process what you feel and then verbally communicate it. When the mental body is overwhelmed or out of balance, persistent anxiety, obsession, compulsive behavior, antisocial behavior, hyperactivity, or hyper-alertness often result.

Throat chakra (fifth chakra): Processes communication and self-expression; governs the throat, thyroid, and hypothalamus. Color: blue.

The third eye or brow chakra (sixth chakra): Processes vision and spiritual perception and governs the pineal gland, thymus gland, and eyes. Color: indigo.

Causal body

The causal body is another name for the spiritual body, but refers directly to the highest or least dense energy that we relate to while we are in our physical bodies. In it is contained many other vibrational layers/levels, but for our purposes here, we are focusing on it as a whole. It is the level of energy that we can connect to via our higher beliefs, philosophies, and ideals; through the causal body we can recognize the presence of angelic beings and other higher vibrational beings that communicate with our world.

In our physical body, the causal body connects to the heart chakra. The Star of David is its symbol, relating to the concept that God lives in the heart. The crown chakra sits just above the head and connects to the pineal gland, a gland that creates a natural chemical called DMT (N,N-dimethyltryptamine) that allows you to have spiritual sight. DMT is a natural hallucinogenic. The causal body also connects to the thymus gland, which has its own chakra just below the heart, located where the xiphoid process is. It connects your soul memory to the physical body and your immune system.

Crown chakra (seventh chakra): Processes higher wisdom, spiritual information, and our connection to other dimensions of energy; governs the brain. Color: purple.

Heart chakra (fourth chakra): Processes the energy of love and compassion and governs the heart and lungs. Color: green.

Soul chakra (ninth chakra): Holds current spiritual imprints of your soul's plan or "destiny." Your destiny may include very specific events that will occur in your life, but predominantly it contains dynamics that will attract to you likely situations and events that are not necessarily "destined." This information governs the thymus gland, which regulates the immune system in the physical body. This chakra is located above the crown chakra. Color: white gold.

How I Met Star Bear

In my early twenties I lived in Harlem and was taking acting classes, Afro-Haitian dance, and waiting on tables at a local Italian café. Actually, I had two apartments: a little room on 110th Street with a fabulous bay window facing Broadway from the second floor above a Korean deli; and, my favorite, a rent-controlled ghetto tenement flat owned by the City of New York. It was a five-floor walk-up I squatted (and paid rent on) until the city gave me a lease. The building was from the 1800s, just at the edge of Central Park and Eighth Avenue. Many of the buildings within a three-block radius were burned out or abandoned and had been taken over by the city from previous owners who owed taxes. When I "moved in," apartment 3R had no windows, meaning the holes were there but no windows. After the courts granted me a lease from the city, they sent a crew to fix things up, and soon I had my very own *Flash Dance* studio, complete with mirror-lined walls. This was not the city's design, of course; it was mine. I made fast friends with the crew, and the lack of supervision allowed me to knock out a wall and make the three-bedroom apartment into a dance studio with a huge walk-in closet, bedroom, kitchen, and bath.

Many of those months were fraught with drama, joblessness, and the taming of all the voices within me—and there were many voices just begging for expression. As a rule, I ate pretty well because I usually had a restaurant job, so weight gain and loss were always a struggle. I'm not gonna lie: I was mad at the world and distraught with grief about every-thing, from having been raped, to the daily witnessing of an ever-growing homeless population in New York City that, it appeared, no one really cared about. I was, however, very inspired to carve out a new life for myself.

It wasn't until I hadn't worked at a food establishment for more than a month that my hunger began to motivate me. Luckily I'd made a few local friends who understood I was living on the emotional edge and really sought to help smooth things out for me. One of these friends was the ironworks foreman who was putting together the structure for the high-rise being built across the street from me. Named Big Red, with Irish red hair and an imposing stature, he was in his late 50s and saw me as his surrogate daughter. Every day that he was on site, around lunchtime the intercom would buzz in my apartment; it was Big Red.

"Your regular lunch order today? We're going to V&T's."

"Yes, Red, thank you," I'd reply and then burst into tears. Usually the tears would clear away by the time my lunch order arrived.

Having worked since I was thirteen, I wasn't used to anyone paying my way for anything—at least that's how I justified my emotional response to someone's kindness, at the time. V&T's had this uncommonly large, oval-shaped hamburger that came with fries. Often, I could get at least two meals out of it. Sometimes I would go downstairs and chat with Red.

He always knew when I'd been crying but never asked about it. He just fed me and talked about current events. I appreciated that.

> No matter what, I'd decided I wasn't having any of that. I needed a job and my strategies hadn't been working, so one vibrant, slightly cool day in October I awoke with the conviction: I was going out, I was going to get a job, and I was not coming home until I did.

I remember the day Star Bear became elevated in my awareness, to more than just a voice of reason and diplomacy. I remember it like it was yesterday. It was a powerful day for me. At that point I hadn't worked in a couple of months and things were becoming dire. Luckily the city was loose on its eviction protocol; otherwise, I would have been out on my nose. No matter what, I'd decided I wasn't having any of that. I needed a job and my strategies hadn't been working, so one vibrant, slightly cool day in October I awoke with the conviction: I was going out, I was going to get a job, and I was not coming home until I did.

I set out walking south on Columbus Avenue, with my last eight dollars in my pocket, hoping to find a job at one of those cute trendy establishments that seemed to be all the buzz. By eleven o'clock a.m. I was having thoughts of what coffee shop might be open twenty-four hours where I may be able to nurse a cup of coffee until the managers came in the next day—although, it was still early in the day. The great thing about New Yorkers is when you ask a straight question, you get a straight answer.

"I'm a waitress, do you have a job for me?"

"No. Good luck."

I had walked sixty blocks so far, and that was the chorus.

The story of Chief Doe-Wah-Jack

It was about three-thirty p.m. and now I was in full contemplation of possible twenty-four-hour coffee shops downtown in case I needed refuge; after all, I couldn't go home. Feeling a little disheartened and a little tired around 27th Street and Seventh Avenue, I spied a bright red *Sale* sign at a little junk shop across the street. Junk on sale—anything on sale for that matter—always cheered me up.

I strolled on over to the sale junk bin in front of the store and saw that the sign said two for five dollars. That was magic to my ears. There were many wonderful things, but the two that caught my eye were a little, brass statue of baby Krishna and a bronze-looking statue of *Chief Doe-Wah-Jack*. For a moment I lost my breath and my heart opened and I didn't feel scared about staying up all night in a coffee shop if I couldn't find a job. The chief was a regal man dressed in ceremonial robes and what looked like a necklace of beads and bear claws.

I knew he was for me.

I bought Krishna for a friend as a gift of gratitude, and I bought Doe-Wah-Jack for me. I ponied up the five dollars, leaving me with three left for that anticipated cup of coffee. I was on my way again. I wondered, *Who was this Doe-Wah Jack?* Holding the little eight-inch statue in hand, I said, "Doe-Wah, I need your help to find a job. I really don't want to be in some seedy coffee shop all night."

Don't get me wrong here. I knew the statue wasn't going to help me but seeing the reflection of this strong, indigenous American man warmed my heart and somehow made me feel safe. And I did have a lot of fun talking to him and introducing him around to all the places I stopped. I know you're probably thinking that's why I didn't get a job—I was introducing statues and all—but he was quite the conversation piece.

Finally, getting into the Village right in between East and West, I was walking on University Place. There weren't a lot of establishments around there, so I was walking at a pretty fast clip when all of a sudden my whole body came to a complete halt, almost as if I'd run into a sliding glass door. It was so abrupt it startled me. I was standing in front of a nondescript black door with a little, black tattered awning that said *Bradley's*. It looked like one of those creepy bars that opened at eight a.m., so I wasn't too eager to breach the doorway. I began to continue down the street and once again hit the glass door, this time laughing at the ridiculousness of it all.

So, with Doe-Wah-Jack in hand, I breached that door and went in, entering a quiet, peaceful little place with charming wooden features, a baby grand piano, and about fifteen tables. There was an old man with platinum hair sitting alone at the bar enjoying his vodka rocks and a short, very thin lumberjack-looking man behind the bar. The two were chatting.

I walked all the way in and sat at the end of the bar nearest the cash register, putting Doe-Wah on the bar next to my folded hands...and waited.

The bartender didn't pay me any mind for a few minutes and then walked over near the register to add a drink to his customer's tally. He then looked over at me and in true New York style said, "Can I get you and your friend a drink?"

We both smiled.

"Well, I'm looking for a job, I'm a waitress. Do you happen to know if there's anything available here? My name is Tracee, by the way."

"I'm Rich," he said. "Why don't I get you a soda while you wait. The manager is in the back, and I'll get her for you?"

"That would be great, thank you. I'll take a Coke," I said while thinking, *I hope you're buying this soda because I might need to buy a cup of coffee later.*

In about ten or fifteen minutes a brilliantly white woman (as pale as I'd ever seen), with fabulous white, eighties hair, who stood about 6'4" with heels, came out of the back office. She was Polish and had a lovely accent.

She said "Hi, you're a *vaitress?*"

I said, "Yes."

She said, "Can you come in and train for lunch tomorrow and then I can put you on the schedule for Thursday, Friday, and Saturday if it works out? The head waitress will be here then."

"That would be amazing," I said with a great sigh of relief.

We both laughed as we realized we hadn't even introduced ourselves. She disappeared into the back office, and Rich and I chatted for a bit.

"Well, it looks like it's your lucky day. Who's your friend here?"

I chuckled and said, "Yes, I see it is, and honestly I have no Idea. I just spent my last five dollars on him, somehow I knew he could help me find a job, and we came right here."

"Well, congratulations," Rich said, "Your drink is on me."

It turns out that little establishment was one of New York City's iconic jazz clubs. People came from all over the world to play and listen to jazz there. The experience was a real game changer for me on so many levels. It was the first place in which I clairvoyantly saw demons on people and was where I cultivated wonderful friendships, some whom I still nurture today.

> THE UNIVERSE IS REPRESENTED IN EVERY ONE OF ITS PARTICLES. EVERY THING IN NATURE CONTAINS ALL THE POWERS OF NATURE. EVERY THING IS MADE OF ONE HIDDEN STUFF; AS THE NATURALIST SEES ONE TYPE UNDER EVERY METAMORPHOSIS.
>
> RALPH WALDO EMERSON

I truly love how spirit works; there are never really coincidences, and everything does in fact happen for a reason. As for Doe-Wah-Jack, it took me some time to understand all of that. In Los Angeles, a colleague of mine channeled for me about Doe-Wah-Jack. The information was a little confusing and unclear. It seemed that he was a chief but that he didn't really live. To me, the statue represented Star Bear, the spirit with whom I communicated regularly. Star Bear did live some time centuries before.

For many years, I tried to find any information I could on either one. It wasn't until literally the writing of this chapter, that I found out the real origin of Chief Doe-Wah Jack. Finally, the chief had become Googleable. Evidently, in the late 1800s, in Dowagiac, Michigan, a wrought iron stove company called Round Oak was founded by P. D. Beckwith, Inc. Chief Doe-Wah-Jack was a fictional Indian chief who appeared on most Round Oak Stove Company advertising and stoves until the company's demise in 1946.

Customers had trouble pronouncing *Dowagiac* so when a prospective customer called and asked the telephone operator for a connection, Chief Doe-Wah-Jack remedied that problem by providing the town's phonetic spelling. I laughed long and hard at that; and even though my statue of Doe-Wah-Jack probably has some antique value, his presence has been invaluable to me. He sits proudly on my altar today in honor of all who have lived before me and a nod to good ol' American marketing.

> Patience and endurance are your two most powerful weapons against a demon. And likewise, they are a demons most formidable tool against you. A demon's nature never changes, however a human being is ever-changing.

The Slayer's Ritual:

Answering Old Questions

What you'll need: white candle, pen, and paper

Sit down in a comfortable place and light your candle. In today's exercise you are going to bring to mind a situation or conversation that you have questions about. You may need to sit a moment and take several deep breaths to relax and allow the information to come forward. Write out all of the questions one by one and then using your imagination answer them. Close your eyes if need be and read your question aloud then answer it with the first thought that comes to your mind. Write what comes to you down on paper.

Don't worry about understanding it just yet; just write down whatever it is because there are no wrong answers. After you've done this with all of your questions, put the paper down and pick it up again at the same time the next day. Reread all of your questions and answers and if more questions arise go through the process again. Keep doing this until you feel complete and that the *door* to that question has been closed.

PART 5
Use It or Lose It

Demons Use Your Desires Against You

The Slayer's Weapons:

Curiosity, Expression, Integration, Boundaries, Patience

Jane Overland: Sleuth of the Mind

No matter what, there is always a sacrifice. To get something better, you must give up something to make room. To find balance, you must give up extremes for moderation, pride for humility, or hunger for fullness. Remember that you can have anything you want, and very possibly, what you have is indeed what you want.

Jane Overland is the psychic investigator that people call upon when they need more understanding and information about themselves, or when they need a strategy in order to transform their situation. What they sometimes don't realize is once they have more information, change is inevitable.

It was almost evening and Jane was getting ready to go to the library when she got the call. Finally, the meeting she'd been fighting for had been agreed to by all the factions that Jane had been working to get together for quite some time. She'd been meeting in secret for several months with each of them. But up until now they'd resisted, showing no interest in coming to the table.

There was a special place out in the high desert, a grouping of trees that had somehow grown out over the years. They bent over each other, almost forming a cave. That's where she met with the Elitists. The power that they possessed was entitlement, a sense of confidence like no others. But Jane knew their attitude was rooted in the fear of losing all they had achieved and sometimes commandeered from others. She hoped that they would someday understand that there was enough for everyone—no matter what. They always met at the midnight hours, and the cave was always lit with a candle or two. Jane never saw their faces, but she didn't need to; she could see their hearts.

She'd meet the Emos in the afternoon at the coffee shop. She could always find them on their computers doing something. It took months for her to convince them that meeting with the other groups could be helpful. (Meeting others made them nervous.) The Emos have a special ability to process many streams of intelligence simultaneously, and because they do it with their minds they can get overwhelmed with other emotions very easily.

The Goths were always a little interested, even though they masked it well while in the presence of Jane. They just never seemed to get up before three p.m. and frankly didn't think anyone cared—objectivity wasn't their specialty. Jane thought they were so artistic and visionary, and she really appreciated their ability to see to the core of a matter. Their vision could take them far past the trivial details into the origins of a pattern. Because of that, they were always really serious most of the time.

The Regulars, believe it or not, were the last to agree to the meeting. First of all, they didn't think they needed to meet the others—after all, *what could any of them do for us,* they thought. On the surface, the Regulars were all pretty good at most things and didn't really think they needed anyone. They had a pretty good sense of humor and addressed most situations with a rationale. But after months of Jane's perpetual, penetrating questions they came to realize that underneath it all they were just a little scared of the others. To the Regulars, they always seemed so dramatic. As it turns out, fear was the one common denominator that they all shared.

> To find balance, you must give up extremes for moderation, pride for humility, or hunger for fullness.

The meeting was set. They wanted to have it at a funeral home.

Hmm, Jane thought. "Well, why don't we meet at my house? It's pretty close to a funeral home—complete with dead people, a few urns, some large trees, and a garden."

Everyone called her home *Jane's House of Happy,* and it made them all laugh a little. They thought Jane was a bit silly. She was always so inspired and positive, traits that the rest of them didn't quite trust in. So that was another thing they found they had in common: they could make fun of Jane.

The only meeting time they could all agree upon was dusk. It wasn't light or dark, they would all be able to see each other clearly, and depending on the weather, maybe they'd get a golden hour. It seemed that all of them were reluctantly looking forward to this meeting.

Jane was a unique bird herself: pale skin with a short, blunt haircut; auburn-brown hair; a waif-like figure; and she didn't seem to have a lot of sexuality about her. Even when she wore her customary plaid miniskirt that was very short, people paid more mind to the huge, round glasses she wore that made her look like she was in a fish bowl.

Jane could talk to anyone, and no one ever felt judged. She enjoyed using her intense curiosity, clairvoyant visions, telepathy, faith, and determination to help bring people to a common understanding of one another. That was always the goal. She would have her work cut out for her with this group. These were all the power factions that had been vying for control for years. They all had such deep ideals and beliefs yet lacked the true meaning behind those beliefs, and now it was time to come to an understanding.

The Elitists knew of man's entitlement to God's kingdom, to God's power, and his mercy. However, over the years that sense of entitlement became arrogance and ignorance. Somewhere along the line they began to believe that they were the only ones with this entitlement and that they were not only different from the others but actually supreme over all others. This illusion became the wedge that ignited their separation from God. It lead to choices that overlooked the needs of everyone except their own. Soon there was nothing but a constant struggle and fight with everything and anyone. That's why they preferred the darkest hours.

The Emos knew that they had access to all God's information at all times. They were crazy smart. The problem was they didn't really trust anyone at all. They knew they were different and didn't really care to deal with authority. Interaction with the others gave them a lot of anxiety because they had difficulty processing their feelings through empathy. So they kept to themselves, and soon they became isolated and alone. This illusion became the wedge that ignited their separation from God. After all, what good is amazing intelligence and infinite access if you can't share it with others?

The Goths had rivers that ran deep. They were feeling and creative and just knew they were different. All they wanted was to express themselves, be accepted, and embraced. They received God's vision and felt sad most of the time because to have such penetrating awareness all

155

the time could be such a burden, especially at the beginning. This illusion became the wedge that ignited their separation from God. The more they believed that no one understood, the more they lost the understanding of God's vision.

The Regulars were…well, they were just regular. They didn't really care about much except what affected them. They were focused on getting what they needed for themselves, and really not much else, overlooking the needs of others. A strong work ethic was their biggest attribute, but soon their ambition became the wedge that ignited their separation from God. Stepping over people or harming them to get what you need produces a significant amount of damage over time to both a spirit and its family not yet born.

It was the night of the full moon, thirty minutes before dusk. The Emos were the first to arrive. Jane had set up a circle of five chairs around a large wooden table out under the largest oak tree in the garden, and each of the groups sent its leader. The table was covered with a black cloth and in front of each chair was a colored candle along with a special crystal. The rising moon was already visible in the sky.

The Emo leader sat in the chair with the indigo candle and a soothing piece of fluorite. Next to arrive was the leader of the Regulars; he sat in the chair with the yellow candle and a piece of citrine. Two minutes after the appointed time, in strolled the leader of the Elitists, sitting at the chair with a green candle and a piece of rose quartz. Finally, rushing in a little late, was the leader of the Goths. She sat at the place with a red candle and a beautiful piece of carnelian.

Jane addressed the group: "Over the last several months I have listened intently to each and every one of your groups' desires, hopes, struggles, and fears. So this meeting isn't to further hear you out. It is to tell you all of your profound value. I have spent time investigating each of you and find that it is fear that bonds you to one another, the belief that you need no one else or that there is no one else who understands you. Your fear of not being accepted for who you are is your lowest common denominator. So, I wanted to give each of you my full report.

"I know when you asked me to look into things you were expecting me to come up with reasons why each of you were better and more valuable than the others—even though you knew deep down that I couldn't.

"Elitists: You are the heart of the group. Indeed, your power can serve everyone. It is true that the heart is the bodily place God can fully speak to, but what has been lost over your generations is the knowledge that fully understanding and interpreting the word of God is impossible without the mind of Emo, the empathy and vision of Goth, and the right and focused action of Regular.

> We all have personality aspects that function as tools to help us in different situations.

"None of you were created to act independently—ever. You need each other, because alone you cannot prosper. I mean really, what good is it to know what to do and be unable to do it? Each of you is an aspect of love that when combined makes this love impenetrable; when all of you contribute who you are to the whole, things move with power, harmony, and a light that eliminates darkness.

"So this is how it's going to be: Elitists, because you are the most powerful, you will need to consult the Emos and the Goths before taking any directive to the Regulars for action. Is that understood?"

The leader of the Elitists wept for a moment then spoke, "I understand; thank you."

The Goth's leader walked over, placed a hand on the Elitist's shoulder, and said, "I understand."

The leader of the Regulars nodded in agreement, and was ready to go. He motioned to the leader of the Emos, making him a little nervous.

The Regular said, "Why don't we take these crying ladies out for a beer?" Looking at the leader of the Elitists, he said "Would that be all right with you?"

"I think that would be just fine," she replied.

Your Personality and the Devil

Demons use separations in your personality and inner conflicts you may have to cause further division and chaos within you. We all have personality aspects that function as tools to help us in different situations. At times these aspects of our personalities can become split from the main personality and create an additional *alter*, which is an aspect of the personality that appears to be separate or at least function separately from the original personality. The creation of an alter can happen as a result of trauma or imbalance on the physical, emotional, mental, or spiritual level.

A personality split looks and feels different than any sort of possession or spiritual intrusion by an entity. However, some people can have extreme barriers between personalities. For example, one aspect of the personality might function while the person is not consciously aware of it and may have no direct memory of what it said or did. When this is the case, it's not uncommon for an aspect of the personality to have some sort of spiritual attachment as well.

Let the integration begin

Friendships and relationships are a major part of how we learn about ourselves because we are mirrored in others. It's part of the reason why the first five minutes of any relationship is amazing: you are falling in love with yourself all over again, from a new vantage point—unless, of course, you don't like yourself very much, in which case things will always be a bit of a struggle.

What we believe, or are comfortable with about ourselves, is the lens with which we will see others. When we limit ourselves, we limit others. It is through our relationships that we begin to integrate any distinct personalities that we may have. The more people we meet, or the more experiences that we have, the more we can consolidate and integrate our personality (tools) and the resources that we need to experience life in a balanced way. As this integration of aspects of our personality takes place, our beliefs must change as well.

We will eventually learn to expand our limiting beliefs, our all-encompassing (but still exclusive) opinions of ourselves or others. If you use any sentence that starts with, *I always, I'll never, They always, They all,* or *They'll never,* then anything that follows that phrase in a sentence is most likely untrue or unproven. We find this phenomenon often in regards to beliefs about race, ethnicity, nationality, religious affiliation, gender identification, sexual orientation, and socioeconomic status.

People can have different personality alters, some of which are vulnerable to demonic influence. It is not uncommon for a person to have one aspect of their personality vulnerable to a spiritual affliction. The longer a demon can keep you confused about who you are and your value, as well as about the limitations, possibilities, and value of others, the longer that demon has access to you and your power.

However, it is my experience that we are all given vulnerabilities and strengths that will always balance each other out. Vulnerabilities are areas of our personality and spiritual makeup where we are able to receive new information outside our lowest common denominator. These areas, unfortunately, often have pain or disempowered memory attached to them. This new information, once the pain has been grieved, will be the key to transforming old, unwanted energy patterns that cause discordant behavior, feelings, and emotional reactions.

Ultimately, it is your spiritual goal to use your inherent personality traits, skills, tools, and abilities; or to innovate them to the point of usefulness, creating balance on all levels of your life. While it may appear at times that the deck is stacked against you, you've been given all the cards necessary to win every hand you've been dealt.

> HE WHO OVERCOMES OTHERS IS STRONG; HE WHO OVERCOMES HIMSELF IS MIGHTY. HE WHO IS SATISFIED WITH HIS LOT IS RICH; HE WHO GOES ON ACTING WITH ENERGY HAS A FIRM WILL.
>
> LAO TZU

Never underestimate your ability to say one thing and do another

Everybody has a soft underbelly—you know, that part of your feelings that is so true you want to protect it with everything you have. Energetically, in the aura it is often these feelings that are most present or obvious. Interestingly enough, these feelings are there to protect your deepest, truest desires.

For a couple of years I went through some deep transformations in my relationships; there were quite a few people in my daily physical life who were actually in conflict with me. (Well, more accurately, they were in conflict with themselves.) In objective truth, they weren't my friends; they were acquaintances or associates with whom I had many things in common. Calling our relationships *friendships* was my subjective perspective. With many of them, it was all about what they needed from me, or my availability to them, or even what I had been to them in the past; but these relationships didn't really include who I am as an individual and what I needed today.

During this time I was covered in a shroud of bitterness about my relationships. Always frustrated and defeated, my mantra was, *I don't really have any friends...well, just you. You're my one friend.* I used to say this a lot. Every time, it gave me a chuckle; somehow it felt soothing for me to say. The fact was it always seemed I had quite a few friends and certainly had more of a social life than I could handle.

As I became aware of this mantra, I began to question what it reflected. I prayed on it every night: "God, why do I feel this way?"

As it turned out, for me this was the end of a very long cycle of living a particular energy pattern. Being in the helping business had surrounded me with people who hadn't yet fully accepted themselves, and I found out I hadn't really been truly myself in any relationship for quite some time—if ever. I found that I didn't always respond with *my* voice; I responded with the helping voice of what they needed.

There was definitely an unintegrated opinion that was present most of the time. You can't be a powerful diplomat if there is no truth to your diplomacy. There was how *I felt*, and then what *I said*; and they were often different. As I began to bear down on this idea, I noticed that I was using my mantra with mainly a couple of people. One was a gal I spoke with often, we'd known each other over a decade at that point. I considered her to be a close friend at the time, and at least once per conversation my mantra would come up.

"I don't really have any friends...well, just you. You're my one friend." (Chuckle.)

I really needed to get at what this was about for me. I was getting tired of my mantra. I started to recognize that my life was filled with acquaintances, people with whom I had some sort of professional relationship that led to the deep spiritual connection allowing me to do my work. I didn't feel I could really be myself most of the time. There was always a time, a day, or a conversation when for the sake of the other person I deliberately avoided saying or doing what I really felt or wanted.

Whoa, what a revelation. It was awful—and awfully sad. It appears I hadn't been completely honest with myself. So I began to pray on that.

Lord, help me be myself, and gracefully be at peace with the consequences.

I knew there would be consequences, for what usually comprised other peoples' outer circle was exactly what made up my inner circle... or really my entire circle. Maybe it's better to say it this way: I treated everyone with the same deep regard because I knew them all in such a deep spiritual way since it was my nature to know their deepest secrets. I think that I thought they knew me in the same way and with the same understanding—or at least cared to.

However, that was not the case. Nor should it have been. I was the only one that needed to get on board with what was happening as opposed to what I wanted to be happening.

Finally, one day this friend I spoke of just decided to abandon ship— literally. She just stopped calling or responding, without a conversation or a warning. After about two weeks of her responding with curt, subtle rejections or not at all, I finally asked, "Hey, what's going on?"

Her response astounded me.

It had been a really powerful time for me, as a relationship dynamic that I'd constantly found myself in was coming to a profound and chaotic close. It was marked by the end of a romantic relationship that was unsalvageable. This was not a huge surprise as he was one of the people who really had a difficult time with me just being myself. We were in conflict most of the time, but to me no relationship is unsalvageable and that kept me attached to the relationship. One of the hardest lessons I had to learn was that I must accept things exactly as they are before any real change can happen, and sometimes that change is making the decision to find peace and completion in just walking away. No conversation, no diplomacy or negotiation, no settlement—just pure abandonment.

I understand what a toll a breakup can have on your friends and loved ones when you share it with them. What was interesting about this friend with whom I'd had daily conversations was that in spite of not speaking with her about him she just decided to turn away from me because she didn't like the man I'd been involved with. That was it and we didn't speak again for over a year.

On one level I was heartbroken but on another I wasn't really too sad about it. I noticed within a little over a week that I hadn't used my mantra at all. I no longer felt I didn't have any friends, and while she was such a substantial part of my daily life, I realized that I had always taken a more altruistic approach to our relationship and was never completely truthful about my opinions with her. Mostly we spoke of general topics as opposed to deeply personal ones. I'd always just supported her and her decisions, not really considering to give my opinion, concerned that it might be hurtful at times. In friendships I have the intrinsic belief that unless the way a person lives is hurting me, my opinion isn't always necessary unless it's asked for. So, I never really expressed it. But knowing that she could not offer me the same...wow, what a load off. I felt relieved and joyful that any further relationship with her could only foster honesty in any possible future.

> You can't be a powerful diplomat if there is no truth to your diplomacy.

Our spirits work in amazing ways. I learned that real friendships are cultivated in sometimes painful honesty and that I needed to spend more time cultivating my personal, subjective opinion. I needed to pay more attention to myself, my inner dialogue, and in some instances my outer dialogue so that my spirit could tell me everything I needed to know.

The Slayer's Path: To Think and Feel

Negative thoughts have a positive message

The slayer's path is to think and feel—always—but also to cultivate the ability to think and feel with honesty, mastery, and flow. Sometimes, when we don't like what we think and feel, we naturally stop the flow so that we may better and more clearly recognize what we are thinking and feeling. Does it make you mad that sometimes your thoughts are really negative? Most of us have spent a good part of our lives and energy feeling angry, sad, and ashamed of these thoughts and their role in our lives. Little time is spent on acknowledging their nature, function, and purpose.

Demons are dense in nature and can connect to all of our lower vibrational emotions such as anger, grief, sadness, greed, lust, guilt, disappointment, or apathy, to name a few. Although we consider these emotions to be negative, it is the very nature of that negativity that allows for the presence of their positive message in our physical world. They are potent enough to penetrate the physical world we live in and are the anchors connecting all other creative energy here. Essentially, all of our negative thoughts hold great power for each and every one of us in the true message that they bring.

Negative thoughts are arrows that have a very important function in our world; they are as incredibly transformative to us as a chisel is to stone. They have an equal and opposite value that is positive. Every thought has a negative or positive vantage, and that means every negative thought has a positive meaning. While a demon's purpose is to create chaos and destruction, chaos in and of itself is not bad; in fact, chaos is a very necessary part of the natural cycle of all things and a universal truth.

The Slayer's Path: **To Think and Feel**

Take the emotion of bitterness, for example. Bitterness exists in place of heartfelt communication. When the throat (fifth) chakra is out of balance, the heart doesn't get enough of the flow it needs for balance. My bitterness about my relationships existed because I had been in a therapeutic (spiritual) outlook (lens) regarding almost every person that I knew, professionally or personally. I now had personal needs (sacral, solar plexus, and heart chakras) that weren't getting any attention from me because for so many years my focus was on my work and on learning my craft.

Over time I didn't make the adjustments I needed in myself, or communicate my needs to the people who were most important to me. In fact, I'd not really made any distinction at all. My lens in all my relationships had been from the place of compassion, a spiritual vantage (heart, third-eye, and crown chakras), wherein the truth is we are all equal and have immense value. My truth, for many years, was that my needs were fulfilled just by helping, that helping others helped me. When that dynamic changed, when I realized that helping others didn't necessarily always help me, I didn't make the necessary adjustments to solidify the new dynamic.

> FOR MEN AND WOMEN TO MEET FREELY AS MATURE AND INTEGRATED PEOPLE, THEY EACH HAVE TO LIVE IN UNISON WITH THEIR INNER OPPOSITE SEX, FOR WOMAN CAN ONLY TOUCH THE ESSENTIAL BEING OF A MAN IF SHE HAS INTEGRATED HER INNER MAN, AND A MAN WILL ONLY REACH THE TRUE BEING OF A WOMAN IF HE HAS INTEGRATED HIS INNER WOMAN.
>
> MARIE-LU LORLER,
> *SHAMANIC HEALING WITHIN THE MEDICINE WHEEL*

A slayer must learn to become all things to themselves, rendering them invincible. When we believe that we are not whole without the presence of others, we become vulnerable to the pursuit of those needs that we cannot meet by ourselves. Consciously or unconsciously we seek to fulfill our needs in the world outside of us. When we do that, we diminish our own sense of power, self-trust, and faith, which are the three most important characteristics of a slayer. As you begin to become all things to yourself, you will be able to love completely and find love in every circumstance. The Mesoamerican and Huna philosophies of the *nagual* (Na'hual) and the three aspects of self beautifully describe how we communicate and relate to ourselves and others.

> What you are surrounded by you will become or it will become you.
>
> Jane Overland

The Spiritual Aspects Of Yourself

The nagual

Nagual has many definitions and comes from the Nahuatl language spoken by the Aztec and many of their predecessors. It defines everything from the idea of charisma to the ability to shapeshift or a person's relationship with their animal totem.

The aspect that I am focusing on today is the nagual (n'hual) as every man and woman's relationship with their inner opposite. (The nagual is also referred to as *anima* and *animus* in modern psychology.) When two people meet, it is each person's nagual that meet first. The nagual is an unconscious or invisible dynamic of connection, which establishes the initial pattern of relating that will either need to be supported or redesigned within the relationship.

Often, a person seeks a relationship partner who expresses aspects of their nagual in the *tonal*—the physical world and all that it's connected to. That means that a woman is attracted to a man who expresses her inner masculine self. The nagual and tonal are the two that make up the whole: the visible and invisible.

The Slayer's Motto: I Am All Things to Myself

A significant factor in how we address our relationships is explained by a basic principal of shamanism: the four shields of the self or the axis of the nagual. A man's nagual is made up of the four shields of his inner essence: his inner grown woman and inner female child, and his inner grown man and inner male child. A woman's nagual is her inner grown man and inner male child, and her inner grown woman and inner female child. Every person must find, balance, and then integrate these four aspects of him- or herself. Without that integration, it is natural to seek your inner selves in the people you attract and relate to.

The day Kelly walked into my office, she was distraught. A beautiful, very slight, and delicate young lady in her mid-twenties, she'd been dating a man who was much older, and the relationship had become quite intense. Kelly told me that when they met there was a huge attraction; she thought he was a very spiritual man, and that's what she was looking for.

They'd only been dating a few months but he was getting really obsessive and controlling. She'd been giving him mixed messages by pulling away emotionally but staying in the relationship and not communicating. Naturally this triggered his insecurity and he'd been emotionally, mentally, and spiritually focusing on her every waking moment they weren't together. Every night he was in her dreams, and it was scaring her. She wasn't getting any sleep at all when she wasn't with him. The final straw, the thing that made her come see me, was that she'd gotten up in the morning to take a shower and saw his face in the shower door even though he wasn't physically there. She burst into tears. He just wouldn't let her be. She couldn't even take a shower without his presence.

The Slayer's Motto: **I Am All Things to Myself**

The first thing I did for Kelly was reassure her she wasn't losing her mind. It seems her boyfriend comes from a culture where magical practices are common. I suspected he was insecure, fearful of losing her, and focusing all of his energy and attention on her, maybe using rituals, maybe not, but it didn't matter. He said he loved her, but his fear of losing her or being abandoned wouldn't let him truly love her. She'd told him she needed some time to herself, but the energy intrusions only became more forceful. He was certain she was cheating on him.

She asked if I had any sort of spell, any reversal ritual I could give her, to fend off his psychic attack. I explained to Kelly that because she'd entered into the situation, that she was empowered to resolve it. Doing battle on the energy level is the same as having a fight in the physical world. It comes down to a battle of wills, but with one very important distinction. What Kelly was doing was as vital and powerful to him as the energy he was sending to her. For some underlying reason, Kelly was frightened and pulling away without saying anything to him about it, and this gap in their communication left him to figure it out on his own, which was creating the path for the surge of his psychic investigation.

Kelly had two options: she could try to match his forces in the spirit world using her energy and intention, or she could just have an honest conversation with him. She could let go of feeling victimized and decide that she wasn't going to participate at all in the battle on the psychic wavelengths. I suggested that going toe-to-toe with him in the spiritual world would only bring her more strife and explained that he could only have the control over her mind, body, or spirit that she gave him.

I also explained that the fact she had attracted such a spiritually proficient man was an indication of her telepathic abilities as well and she could speak telepathically to him, asking him to stop the intrusions. I told her that love is about respect on all levels, and that if he loved her he needed to find a way to respect her wishes and give her space. But if she really wanted to leave no option for misinterpretation, then she must have a direct, verbal conversation. Bringing the spiritual dynamic into the physical realm stops the psychic path of communication, at least for a time.

My final thoughts to Kelly were that if she addressed the situation with compassion, it would resolve more quickly. I saw Kelly approximately three more times, supporting her through her transformation. Finally, after many meditations on her part—gathering, centering, and empowering herself— the boyfriend broke up with her, saying he wasn't getting what he needed. She was quite relieved but grateful for having learned so much about herself in the process.

Huna

One of the most practical explanations I've ever heard to explain the dynamic of how we spiritually integrate ideas and communicate with ourselves through the process of creating something in the physical world, is in a book called *Kahuna Magic,* by Brad Steiger. The book is centered on the original work of Max Freedom Long and his beliefs about the kahunas of Hawai'i. Basically the principal is this: We all have a lower self, middle self, and higher self. When any idea, feeling, or opportunity is generated, it is first integrated by the low self (the subconscious), which pulls up any information (memories, emotions, support, or obstacles) that need to be processed by the middle self (the conscious mind), and then at this time the middle self can access the higher self for information and strategy regarding how to complete the transformation into manifesting the idea.

Intentions are good, understanding is better

Robert didn't understand why when he asked the universe for more money and a better job that his whole life seemed to blow up. He lost his job and his relationship. Going through a pending divorce, he sought my help. He was experiencing extreme confusion, grief, and frustration regarding how to get his life back on track. He was feeling punished and didn't know why all of this was happening to him.

As we began to talk, it all made perfect sense. He hadn't been happy for a long time. He and his wife had been in a struggle with her alcoholism; she didn't believe she had a problem. He was doing work that he loved, but it was fraught with conflict and he was not paid a lot of money. As we began to deconstruct the situation, everything seemed to have begun about a year before when he accepted how unhappy he was and decided he couldn't live like that anymore. He began focusing his intentions by writing in his journal, asking the universe to help him find a better job with more money.

I explained that everything that was happening was right on time. When you want to make extreme and far-reaching change in your life, oftentimes everything in your life—everything based on your beliefs, thoughts, and expectations—now must change. Everything that was created with them will also change. In this case, everything included Robert's marriage, job, body, mind, and spirit. If he was going to let go of his wife and her addiction, then he would have to let go of any addictive behaviors he had.

We were then able to uncover some past-life patterns in his participation in a dominant/submissive relationship in which he had been quite cruel and abusive to his partner. It echoed the dominant/submissive relationship that he now had with his wife, where he was now in the submissive role. The spiritual intent was not to punish him for past-life transgressions, but to liberate him from the pattern completely by allowing him to have full-circle understanding. With this information he was able to find a deep sense of forgiveness for himself and his wife and to heal the spiritual pattern that created it all. That was the real turning point for him and the creation of a new life.

MY SONS, IF YOU ARE OF ONE MIND, AND UNITE TO ASSIST EACH OTHER, YOU WILL BE AS THIS BUNDLE OF STICKS, UNINJURED BY ALL THE ATTEMPTS OF YOUR ENEMIES; BUT IF YOU ARE DIVIDED AMONG YOURSELVES, YOU WILL BE BROKEN AS EASILY AS A STICK WHEN IT IS SEPARATED FROM THE BUNDLE.

THE FATHER TO HIS SONS, IN AESOP'S FABLES

How I Met Jane Overland: Private Eye

I was about a year into working as a spiritual empath when one night I had a dream where I was staying at the most elegant, beautiful, and ancient-feeling hotel, somewhere in view of the Taj Mahal. The décor was all very dark woods, rich reds, and golds with two sweeping staircases on either side of the huge lobby. In the center was an extravagant front desk with a lavish chandelier dangling from the ceiling. It seemed that it was in a modern time. At midmorning, I was called down from my room to take a call at the front desk. The call was coming from a publisher in Great Britain; the caller asked to speak with Jane Overland, which was me.

She was the writer, the one within me with the curious mind and the objective perspective and a plain and simple way of communicating. It was true that up until this point I had only made jokes of writing a book. I had so many thoughts running in my head at the time, and while I definitely had the most masterful handle on all the people in contact with my spirit that I'd ever had, I didn't sleep too much or too well, and getting a coherent thought down on paper seemed almost impossible. The most writing I did was documenting and analyzing my dreams or occasionally expelling an angry or grief-stricken rant in a paragraph or two.

The thought of writing was magical, but the act of writing was mystical and always eluded me. Jane Overland, however, had quite a command of her thoughts and words. Her frame was slight, and she stood about five feet six inches. She had rich brown hair cut bluntly just past her earlobes, and she wore large, round spectacles that made her eyes seem large and round. Her standard dress was a short green, blue, pink, and black plaid pleated skirt with an untucked white blouse, black tights, and black leather ankle boots. While she definitely had a school-girl-sexy thing happening, it was hard to tell whom she favored, as she responded to everyone just the same. Jane always had a back pack with her, which seemed to have anything you might need in it. She was an interesting, spry, petite young lady who, in spite of her fragile demeanor, was really quite rugged. Jane Overland was a personality blueprint that carried the best traits of my ancestry, my spirit, and my look. I was going to have to learn her ways.

I was in my late twenties when I began a massive soul and person-ality overhaul. The first thing that spirit led me to do was to heal the relationship with my mother. I think that she and I had the most ideal relationship we could've possibly had as we always had a quiet under-standing of each other. She mentioned to me often throughout my life what a good baby I was and that, as a child, I never needed extra attention. So, what arrived at puberty was a vindictive inability to hide my emotions in the way I always had from earliest childhood.

Sun in a sad house

The sun had risen, but the room was still dimly lit with a slight crack of sun streaming over my crib. I was about two years old. The room was filled with sadness from an unknown source. I was always aware of it in that house. People ask me all the time when I knew I was psychic, or if something specific happened to me to make me this way. The truth is I just thought of it as *the* way. I am not sure I understood that not everyone had the level of sensitivity I did. It is strange to think back on my childhood and the extreme awareness I had of myself, others, and my environment coupled with no verbal skills. It was very painful for me not to be able to communicate with those around me, although I didn't cry a lot at the time.

Nightmares and demonic attack plagued my dream hours all through my early years, but the nighttime crying didn't come until I was five or six years old. Even so, night was my favorite time. I would go to bed as early as the sun would let me, sometimes tossing and turning myself into good dreams and sometimes crying myself to sleep. No one ever knew. Well, everyone knew if I'd tossed and turned the night before because my hair would be in knots in the morning, but other than that no one knew. This pattern continued all through high school: experiencing deep and prophetic dreams in my night hours followed by *kriyas* of emotion that gave way to confidence and anxiety during the day.

Taking a leadership role in my life and school activities was the only comfortable way for me, as I felt extremely isolated from anyone who I thought could possibly share or understand my experiences of hearing, seeing, and channeling energy. It wasn't something that even occurred to me to talk about. It was just the secret I shared with the Creator.

Growing up in New Mexico, there was so much pain in the land. Generations of suffering packed in every layer of dirt. I could feel all of it at times with the clarity of a native tracker, and it overwhelmed me, but equally it inspired me, calling my soul to return home. Home is a reckoning of all the places and ways of my spirit, bringing them all back to this one time and space that I call Tracee Dunblazier.

> TO THOSE WHO ARE GOOD TO ME, I AM GOOD; AND TO THOSE WHO ARE NOT GOOD TO ME, I AM ALSO GOOD; AND THUS ALL GET TO BE GOOD. TO THOSE WHO ARE SINCERE WITH ME, I AM SINCERE; AND TO THOSE WHO ARE NOT SINCERE WITH ME, I AM ALSO SINCERE; AND THUS ALL GET TO BE SINCERE.
>
> LAO TZU

The Slayer's Pact: Be a Friend

Being a slayer puts you in the unique position of having a lot of instinctive information about the people that you meet. You may know or learn things about them that you don't like or agree with, but you must find compassion and kindness in spite of your own feelings and opinions. It is possible to set boundaries in your relationships without allowing your judgment to inspire fear or diminishing another person's character. Being an ultra-aware person puts you in a profoundly powerful position; if you're there, you've earned that awareness in some way. Remember, you can take authority over yourself, spiritual influences, and situations, but you can never take authority over other people, even if it appears that for a time you can. Ultimately, that illusion will only create anger and dissent towards you.

Friendships and relationships are the way we learn to take care of ourselves, the way our universe mirrors back to us our most vital information. It's a popular sentiment to consider that taking care of yourself first is selfish, but in fact it is the opposite. You cannot truly take care of others if your own needs are not met, and it is not the responsibility of others to meet your needs. Meeting your needs is only your responsibility, just as it is not your responsibility to meet the needs of others.

The Slayer's Pact: **Be a Friend**

It is, however, your responsibility to teach your friends and loved ones how to treat you. You do this by allowing them to witness your own self-honesty and treatment. For every uncomfortable situation you find yourself in, there is a deeper truth being reflected in you regarding your relationship with yourself. A slayer will always find a way to be good to himself and others.

The Slayer's Altar:
Unity

What you'll need:

- Five three-inch jar candles: white, black, green, yellow, and red
- Paper and pen
- A bowl of tobacco for an offering of gratitude

Sit down with the paper and pen and get comfortable, taking a few deep breaths. Ask yourself, *Who are the main aspects of my personality?* Ask for their names, or give them names. You'll be surprised how easily and quickly this information will come.

Now, ask each aspect of your personality, *What is your function? What exactly do you do for me?*

Write down all of this information on the paper; fold the paper in half and then in half again. Place it under the green candle in the center of your altar; then place the other four candles around the green one. Say a prayer of unity. You may use one of your own or use the one provided here (and feel free to make any changes you want).

Mother Father God

It is my deepest desire to express all that you are within me. Show me the best way to honor my vulnerabilities, for they echo your love and are the channel through which you speak to me. Show me how to fully embrace my strengths, for they are your arms in the world. Most of all show me how to love and accept others in the way I love and accept myself.

Epilogue

The sacred essence of our lives connect across time. Linked by a primeval existence that reverberates at the very core of who we are, taking us on a journey of the ages. Now that we've walked with one another on the red road, I hope you see it fit to say, "I'm a little more at peace with change." That you recognize fear at your back door and not your front. And, that you embrace the human race, Mother Earth that sustains us all, the universe we all live in, and The Creator of whom we are all creations made of One Love.

Demon slaying is not just for warriors, as we are all warriors for love in our own way. Whether you are a watcher or a slayer; your presence, contribution, and affect on others and this planet is indisputable and invaluable. You have power beyond the limits of our current cultural understanding and are learning to embrace it at a very unique period of time with billions of other people in tow.

Science has now proven many things, first that our brain changes continually based on our thoughts and behaviors. Second, that emotions promoted by cultural beliefs have a defined and palpable impact on our physical health. And, third, that we are not relegated solely to the pattern or life condition that our DNA would suggest. With all of the new and profound information available it is not a stretch to embrace that we are impacted by the life and health of our planet or that it is impacted by ours. Or, that we see, feel, and hear the vibrations of a soul essence before our bodies send the signal to the brain to let the eyes know to see the body attached. It makes the existence of bigotry in any form, parochial. The implications of this truth on the hearts of many is life transforming. The opportunity to be personally responsible and accountable for all of the information that you communicate to others and the universe, long before you even speak or are visually seen; is penetrating.

The power that this truth endows is all yours to wield. Not just against something, but *for* something. The more you use your power towards the creation or transformation of what fills your heart, the more it brings peace to your mind and your world. Slaying your demons becomes simple with this understanding. The fight and struggle is not with the demon at hand it is with your fear that the demon promotes. No fear: no demon. All love.

Bibliography

Dale, Cyndi. *The Subtle Body: An Encyclopedia of Your Energetic Anatomy*. Boulder, CO: Sounds True, 2009.

Gerber, Richard. *Vibrational Medicine: The #1 Handbook of Subtle-energy Therapies*. 3rd ed. Rochester, VT: Bear & Company, 2001.

Gladwell, Malcolm. *The Tipping Point: How Little Things Can Make a Big Difference*. New York: Back Bay Books/Little, Brown and Company, 2002.

Glynn, Ian. *An Anatomy of Thought: The Origin and Machinery of the Mind*. Oxford: Oxford University Press, 1999.

Hanson, Rick. *Buddha's Brain: The Practical Neuroscience of Happiness, Love, and Wisdom*. Oakland, CA: New Harbinger Publications, 2009.

Hawkins, David R. *Power vs. Force: The Hidden Determination of Human Behavior*. Carlsbad, CA: Hay House, 2002.

Kornfield, Jack. *After the Ecstasy, the Laundry: How the Heart Grows Wise on the Spiritual Path*. New York: Bantam Books, 2000.

Lipton, Bruce. *The Biology of Belief: Unleashing the Power of Consciousness, Matter, and Miracles*. Santa Rosa, CA: Mountain of Love/ Elite Books, 2005.

Lorler, Marie-Lu. *Shamanic Healing within the Medicine Wheel*. Translated by Matt Schulze and Winter Laite. Albuquerque, NM: Brotherhood of Life, 1991.

Martinez, Mario E. *The Mindbody Code: How to Change the Beliefs That Limit Your Health, Longevity, and Success*. Boulder, CO: Sounds True, 2014.

Paulson, Genevieve Lewis. *Kundalini and the Chakras: A Practical Guide—Evolution in this Lifetime*. St. Paul, MN: Llewellyn Publications, 1991.

Restak, Richard M. *The New Brain: How the Modern Age is Rewiring Your Mind*. Emmaus, PA: Rodale, 2003.

Steiger, Brad. *Kahuna Magic*. West Chester, PA: Whitford Press, 1982.

———. *Totems: The Transformative Power of Your Personal Animal Totem*. New York: HarperCollins Publications, 1997.

Wilson, James L. *Adrenal Fatigue: The 21st Century Stress Syndrome*. Petaluma, CA: Smart Publications, 2001.

Permissions

Some quotes required permission to be used in this text. Much effort was made in obtaining the permission of copyright holders of these quotes. I gratefully acknowledge permissions granted to quote from the following:

- Alan Cohen, http://www.alancohen.com/. Used by permission of author.

- Tracy Renee Jones, http://tracyreneejones.com/. Used by permission of author.

- Marie-Lu Lorler, *Shamanic Healing within the Medicine Wheel*, published by the Brotherhood of Life, 2002. Used by permission of publisher.

- Mario Martinez, *The Mindbody Code: How to Change the Beliefs that Limit Your Health, Longevity, and Success*. Used by permission of author.

- Stephen J. Miller, *The Keepers of Mana'an*. Used by permission of publisher.

- Caroline Myss, "Daily Message Archive," http://www.myss.com/library/dailymessage/. Used by permission of author.

- Brad Steiger, *Kahuna Magic*. Used by permission of author.

- Brad Steiger, *Totems: The Tranformative Power of Your Personal Animal Totem*. Used by permission of author.

About the Author

Tracee Dunblazier, GC-C, spiritual empath, shaman, educator, author and speaker is based in Los Angeles, California. Tracee specializes in grief counseling, energy dynamics, Shamanic healing, past life and soul recovery, transition strategy, addiction transformation, and space clearings. In 2015, Tracee founded GoTracee Publishing LLC and BeASlayer.com to publish a new hybrid of self-help memoir.

As a multi-sensitive, Tracee blends information that she receives intuitively with different modalities to create a unique healing plan for each client. Every session is focused on freeing the client from their presenting issue to release, empower, and heal—no matter what the condition. Tracee's compassionate, humorous, down-to-earth style supports and empowers clients as tender topics are addressed during a session.

An accomplished author, Tracee has written two books on the topic of personal soul excavation and deep healing from soul to body. Tracee's published articles cover many subjects related to spirituality and relationships while her blog breaks down current events and daily energy dynamics that everyone experiences. Tracee's been a guest on LA Talk Radio, Om Times Radio, The Outer Limits of Inner Truth and many other radio and television programs speaking on spirituality and sacred ritual practices. Tracee teaches workshops, webinars, and online courses, as well as speaking engagements touching on topics like grief, death & dying, unconditional love, self- acceptance, and healing.

Contact Tracee at www.TraceeDunblazier.com